Escaping the Jaws of Life

A Widow's Journey to Happiness

LORI GODSEY ANZINI

authorHOUSE®

AuthorHouse™
1663 Liberty Drive
Bloomington, IN 47403
www.authorhouse.com
Phone: 1-800-839-8640

Published by AuthorHouse 1/11/2012

ISBN: 978-1-4685-3748-2 (e)
ISBN: 978-1-4685-3749-9 (hc)
ISBN: 978-1-4685-3750-5 (sc)

Library of Congress Control Number: 2011963704

Author's website: www.lorianzini.com

Cover art by Diana Anzini.

Dedicated to Larry,

My beautiful husband,

A gentle man,

Smart, intelligent, and witty,

A follower of science and physics,

Doubter of religion,

The father of my children.

We had a beautiful life together ...

We will be together again!

Contents

Acknowledgments

To my children, **Donné** and **Daniel**, you are my life. I love you no matter what, unconditionally. I never said that to you enough while you grew up. If you had not challenged me with your reactions, I probably would have never finished this book. I know that in your hearts and souls our journey through life together is infinite. There is no end, and you will soon find that out.

To **Diana**, I couldn't have written this without you. Thank you for your amazing support and encouragement. You also were affected by the loss of a brother and a mother. You stood by me and provided positive energies and enthusiasm as I shared my grief with you. You and I have traveled a journey together to find peace with ourselves. Larry is enjoying our travels together. I love you, Diana.

Thank you, **Chris**. You are my life partner now. We will be best friends forever. You have stood back and stayed out of my way as I have been fighting for air. You have been shouting from the shoreline, "Kick, kick, kick!" every time I felt submerged underwater. We have been thrown together spiritually, and you have brought me kicking and screaming every step of the way. I love you.

To my granddaughters, **Haley, Betty,** and **Clara**, you might read this someday and recognize a bit of me in you. I hope you understand that death and surviving are processes of life. Your grandfather, Papa, loved your parents so much. He would be proud of all of you today. Take whatever challenges that are thrown your way during your life here on earth. Recognize them as lessons because we all have them

To **Paul, Karla,** and **Lin**, you have heard my stories and complaints. You have supported me and been my cheerleaders. I'm excited that you too have shared my journey of finding ourselves. Thank you for being patient while your sister grew up. I think I'm almost there! I love you dearly.

And to all parents—a blessing. We have all learned our parenting from different styles, books, and learned behaviors from our parents. The one significant thing that I learned and would hope that all parents who read this would understand that we really have no control over the children we raise. We can only hope for the best and learn to let go when it's necessary.

Esther Hicks and Jerry Hicks, authors of many books on the laws of attraction, have been a big influence on my growth and change.

One significant reading came from a workshop they hosted in Seattle. I found such resonance with it that I would like to share it with you:

Child of mine—I will never do for you that which I know you can do for yourself. I will never rob you of an opportunity to show yourself your ability and talent. I will see you at all times as the capable, effective, powerful creator that you have come forth to be.

And I will stand back as your most avid cheering section. But I will not do for you that which you have intended to do for yourself. Anything you need from me—ask. I'm always here to complement or to assist, I am here to encourage your role, not to justify my experience through you.

—Abraham-Hicks, 1999

Introduction

It has been four years now, after a thirty-six-year marriage. We would have celebrated forty years together on September 11, 2011. He died on September 7, 2007. This year, I turned sixty; he would have been sixty-one. Since he left, my expansion as a human has dramatically unfolded in a very natural way.

I have accepted the fact that life—in all its contrast—has a tremendous ability to remind me that all the beauty I possess inside is always trying to uplift me into my awareness. When I don't see it or I ignore it, I dwell in my mind on guilt, anger, judgment, and opinion. When I do see it and acknowledge it, a certain feeling of "lightness" goes through my physical body. I savor the birds' singing, the bees' buzzing over the flowers in my garden, my cats' begging for the attention of my touch. I seek the deliciousness of my life and those who are within my sphere of being.

My journey has been magnificent. My "knowing" has moved me into a spirituality that I can wear proudly now. All those years of ignoring it have actually allowed me to review it with great enthusiasm. It is healing. It is healthy. I don't wake up with a guilty feeling of "Why me?" … or "Why not me?"

Decades before, Larry had been introduced to a "positive thinking" seminar through his employer. It really stuck with him for several years. We practiced it with our children, taking a more detached role and allowing them to grow as humans. As the years went by, careers realigned, children grew up, and Parkinson's set in for him and affected our lives with new challenges. Those skills of looking at life positively became diminished. It took him more than three years to realize (with my encouragement and insistence) that the doctor was wrong; it wasn't a just a shoulder tweak that needed physical therapy. He wasn't feeling good at work. He got frustrated very quickly, and he felt his boss hated him. This really, really nice guy who never said anything bad about anyone could not tell that he was sick. I could tell that he felt stress from worrying about it. Most men deny that feeling and hold it all in.

Move forward eight years—after battling early-onset Parkinson's disease and removing ourselves to the country into our "retirement house," I found the movie *The Secret* one year before he got really sick. I bought it and brought it home for him to watch. I could tell that he was resigned more to being sick rather than seeing the message that "you are what you think."

After he passed away from the brain cancer, I dwelled in my "widowhood," quietly. Trying to figure it all out, I started journaling. It worked. Then I reviewed *The Secret* and soon found another video called *The Secret Behind the Secret*. It resonated with me. My beautiful husband, love of my life, knew about it, and we tried practicing it early on … but eventually lost touch with it.

I know that grief can be so painful. Death has been all around me since my grandmother died at our dinner table, choking on meat. I was eighteen years old and just watched it happen in slow motion. Then my father died when I was thirty years old; one girlfriend at the age of forty-four; my uncle, aunt, and mother all within three months; my nephew (age twenty-one—suicide);

my mother-in-law; and my husband five months later. Perhaps all those experiences prepared me for my greatest loss.

I know now and appreciate the fact that I can take the time on a daily basis to reflect on all that I have now, meditate on the good, and seek the wondrous.

I have found that I am attracting people of "like minds" into my life now. I have changed significantly. My grown children (my contrast right now) don't like the decisions I am making. Very likely, this expansion of me is significant enough that they can't handle the changed woman they see. I believe they will come around someday ... or not.

So every day I try not to get "into my mind" and think of what people are thinking of me, instead thinking of what I can do for myself and just loving from within. I am finding that I am happier, healthier, and significantly better off than I would be if I got into my pity party of loss.

So that's all of it in a nutshell. I will continue to go dancing, write, listen to music, and find humor in things that make me joyous. And Larry, just in case you are watching—yes, I am having a fine time. Wish you were here!

> *When something bad happens, you have three choices. You can let it define you, let it destroy you, or let it strengthen you.*
> *—Unknown*

CHAPTER 1

The Reality Factor

As I'm driving up the Highway 101 corridor from Garberville to Eureka on an early October morning, I've got the music on loud in our Jeep Cherokee. The ninety-mile drive from our ranch house in southern Humboldt County might be an inconvenience to the "city slickers," as my ranching father-in-law Ray calls them, but when you live up there, it is the main artery to civilization for people living up in "God's country."

When Larry and I built our retirement home in 2002, we knew that we were giving up a lot with our move from the Bay Area. Our grown children and their families were down there. The five-hour drive down Highway 101 to the Bay Area alone is overwhelming to the "country bumpkins" (the name we used to neutralize the "city slickers" remarks my father-in-law always made to us). But you get used to it.

The drive is truly beautiful. You are surrounded by millions of acres of redwood trees. From spring through fall, it is gorgeous

1

there. You can't help but be happy. When winter comes and stays, you always want to get away from the cold, the rain, the storms, the inconveniences of not having electricity for days. In the fall of 2002, our house was completed, and we were living on Larry's social security disability income and meager disability pension from his twelve years of working at a school district. He had to resign; his nervous system just couldn't take it anymore. In April of 1999, he was diagnosed with early-onset Parkinson's disease. He was forty-nine at the time.

I, who have fought my weight all my life but have only gotten nasty bronchitis from time to time and does not have high blood pressure or high cholesterol, take this in stride. You see, I'm a survivor. It comes naturally. I've researched it. I immersed myself on Ancestry.com and learned about it all. The lines that come from both sides of my family are Revolutionary War heroes. One line goes right to the Mayflower families.

But when I finally saw resignation in my love, in my husband's eyes, to the fact that he was *really* sick, not just having a nervous breakdown because of management changes in his employment, that was the moment I knew. *Uh—oh,* I thought, *you signed onto this and you know just what to do.* I talked him into leaving the job, to take a break. When the break had lasted three months and he told me that he still felt off, I took out the disability papers for him and made him sign on the dotted lines. I researched everything to make sure he took full advantage of the programs available to him. I knew from all the years we had been married that he needed to have a source of income that was fundamentally important to him. We were partners in everything. We made our incomes together, threw it into one pot, paid the bills, raised the kids, and went on a few fun vacations together. It really didn't matter. Married, through sickness and health, till death do we part?

So, when all of my significant responsibilities seemed to stop within a period of four months, I figured the universe was telling me something: Get out of town! I had been responsible for my mother and uncle both when they were in a convalescent hospital. They died within three months of each other. I was an elected city council member and the current mayor of the city at the time. I didn't get re-elected, which is unusual for a sitting mayor. I had a job that I loved, working in a school district. I had a total of twenty-two years in two pension plans, but I could not collect anything until I was fifty-five. *Is the universe sending me a message?*

We sold our house near the height of the housing bubble, took the cash, and built our retirement home about nine hundred feet down a dirt road from the house Larry was raised in. The move was an upheaval for his system. I, born a military brat, had learned at an early age that change was good and inevitable. I managed to work out the details in getting our house built. My husband loved watching me manage things, getting the permits through the county, convincing a contractor to meet our deadline by Thanksgiving. We settled down and enjoyed the country.

I tried getting jobs everywhere. My sense of purpose, especially in the career area, had taken a major hit. I tried being a deli-counter person at the local supermarket; that lasted three days. (I don't like potato salad anymore.) Then I worked as an office manager in a chiropractor office, which lasted six months. I was discouraged that I couldn't find employment that was satisfying.

I finally got the message: *Start your own business.* I did, and word got around in southern Humboldt County that I was a computer consultant. It was nice finally pulling that all together. I probably spent more on transportation costs getting to my jobs than I made.

So there we were in a rural, daily routine, growing our own vegetables, and feeding the wild turkeys. Larry would go out into the oaks and cut down limbs that were hanging near the ground for fire protection. We found a doctor in Eureka, a neurologist who worked with him on his medications.

On this particular day, during the drive, I was feeling overwhelmed. I loved the beauty of the forest; I turned off the music and started talking to something. You see, I really didn't believe there was a "god" or anything like that. But I said, "Universe! Please tell me what I need to do to help get Larry into an improved condition. Please show me a way!" For about five minutes, I ranted, saying that I would do anything it took to make him better.

Two days later, Larry and I drove back up to Eureka to see his neurologist for a three-month visit. When the doctor walked into the room to see us, he said, "I am so glad that you are here! I have, fresh off my fax machine and in my hands right now, an inquiry from the University of California at San Francisco Medical Center. Do you want to hear about it? Because I believe you, Larry, qualify for this test on a Parkinson's study."

Larry and I looked at each other. He, with very anxious eyes, looked at the doctor and said, "Well, doctor, let us hear about it." I recognized that at that moment he enunciated the *us;* he didn't say *me.* The doctor proceeded to tell us that the

University of California at San Francisco (UCSF) was having a special blind study for people with Parkinson's. They were looking for candidates who had never had brain surgery and had reached a point of their disease where medication was not as effective; Larry, after approximately twelve years of Parkinson's, would qualify for this study. We asked for the information so we could study it and promised we would call the doctor by the following afternoon.

With excitement, we wondered if this would be the cure for him. Would this put him in the front of the line of people trying to beat this disease? We had spent so much time looking up stem cell, brain implants, and a whole bevy alternative treatments; this one just seemed to drop into our laps.

Larry and I went home, opened a bottle of wine, and celebrated the fact that something was finally coming our way. We talked and talked about it. His only concern about the procedure was that the doctors would bore two holes in the front part of his skull. He said just thinking about it gave him the shivers. We agreed that we would call the neurologist the next day to ask about it.

When we called the next day, the doctor explained that they would fill in the holes with removable titanium disks to protect the brain. Larry's only question about that was, "What if my brain doesn't like the titanium?" When we hung up with the doctor, we talked again about his doubts. I asked him, "Honey, do you want to be in the front of the line, or do you want to wait two to three years down the line for some other magic to come to you?" He called the doctor back and said, "I would like to try to be a candidate in the study."

There were many steps to be taken and many papers to sign relinquishing any rights to recourse if the study didn't work. Our son's wedding occurred shortly after we made that decision, and we shared the news with his wife's family, two of whom were medical doctors or researchers. It was nice to get feedback from them. Larry's first visit with the UCSF study team was in early December. The nice thing about studies like this is that they pay for all the costs, including time and travel.

Trouble started just before his first visit. His father, Ray, was flown down to the Bay Area for emergency heart surgery and had a quintuple bypass. At the same time, his mother was showing signs of illness—we thought it was just stress—while in the Palo Alto hospital, worrying about her husband. A quick visit to the emergency room revealed that she had Stage IV lung cancer. Both of his parents were in the hospital at the same time! His mother, Clara, had never smoked in her life. It was a double whammy to the family. We were all spinning with the chain of events.

We almost canceled Larry's initial appointment because of this, but with encouragement from his sisters, Diana and Louise, who were handling the care of their parents and appointments at the hospital, we took the trip over to UCSF for his initial review.

The process was thorough. He had more appointments, and they flew us to Vancouver, Canada, for a PET scan there; Vancouver University was a partner in this world research. The trip was a nice distraction from his parents' health problems. His dad was recuperating, but his mom was going through radiation. His immediate family had really never had any major health issues before. His dad, Ray, was eighty-two and his mother was seventy-six.

Larry had to have a liver biopsy because of abnormal cysts. He had to have two different biopsies, and when the second biopsy was ordered, I took pause. Was there some kind of message in the fact that he had to have two? With his mother battling the lung cancer treatments, we felt we were on a slippery slope. The UCSF staff wanted to make sure he was cleared so that the study wouldn't be compromised during the two-year period. When Larry entered the out-patient room for the second biopsy, he held my hand tightly and said "Honey, I really hope this is worth it". We went home and waited for the results.

It took about four days until the doctor called us to say that the cysts were benign. Then the results had to be sent to the UCSF study team for review. We were on pins and needles for about a week until we drove down to San Francisco for the final office visit. They had good news, and once all of his health issues were cleared, the study accepted him in as patient number four. They had fifty candidates in the study. This was phase two of a study that could possibly reveal a cure or put a life-altering halt to the degenerating disease. We had hope.

One week before Larry's scheduled surgery, his sisters brought in hospice to handle the end-of-life care for his mother. The bed was set up in the living room of the house. Larry went up to talk to his mother, and she told him she was concerned about his going through with the surgery. Larry came back down, depressed, knowing that her time was not too far away. He said to me, "I only hope that she will be able to see me well and healthy before she passes." That happened. The day he got home, he immediately went up to her, grabbed her hand, and said, "Mom, see? I'm here, and I'm doing fine." One week after his surgery, she left this earth the way she wanted—in her home and on her own terms. I think she knew she was going to see her son again sooner than most of us believed.

> *As a well-spent day brings happy sleep, so a life well spent brings happy death.*
> *—Leonardo da Vinci*

CHAPTER 2

The Last Swan's Song

As I sat at my computer reading one e-mail after another from both of my children, the pain in my heart just ached at reading what they were saying—all the things I anticipated they would say. I know that they are reacting to a sense that I am removing the shrine to their dad. It was our retirement home, but I'm not getting rid of it—just renting it out for extra income.

This was a defining moment. I had shifted and changed. They were complaining that they didn't recognize me as the mother that they knew. I sat back and breathed, thinking, *Wow!* My life was so much more simpler, being the abiding and adoring wife, doing the worthwhile community service projects, maintaining a successful career, paying attention as a parent, keeping my children involved with after-school activities to make them wholesome and healthy adults and citizens, following the rules, staying in line, being responsible, and being a role model for my children. It was not a sacrifice but something I did because my inner being said it was the right thing. There was never a hesitation; I just did what was expected, making sure all those around me were comfortable and happy. But was I? Was I always happy?

It could have been much worse for my kids. I could have divorced like the other couples around us. I could have been seeking *more* happiness then, trying to find the one partner who "rocked my world." Larry did rock my world, but more important, we rocked it together. Maybe being a bit selfish and seeking another path *might* have made me happier—I never thought twice about it. I really never had that chance, nor did I want it. You see, I was happy—very happy.

A thirty-six-year marriage (less four days) ended on September 7, 2007. He died. *My life witness is gone,* I thought. He vaporized in heavy breathing. The air was still and static with his last breath.

He chose the quickest way to his path with honor, courage, and no pain—thank you, hospice. Thank God for hospice! How wonderful they were to help me through the flurry of that ultimate decision he had made to not extend his life with radiation and chemotherapy to give him just two to four more months to live. He made that decision despite his son's begging him to take the radiation to live long enough to see his second grandchild born. Larry, in his dire need to stop the nonsense of fighting a long battle of early-onset Parkinson's, said, "No, thank you, son. I love you." He took the high road. His mind was lucid in the decision, but somewhere, when the glioblastoma multiforme took over, he was also in his own world.

That mid-August day in 2007, when he made that decision, I was driving our Jeep across the Bay Bridge, away from the University of San Francisco. We had just seen a radiologist about alternatives. He took his seat belt off and opened the door to the Jeep. I was driving in the middle lane of the bridge and grabbed him with my right hand, managing to keep the Jeep in the lane.

"*Larry!*" I yelled with fright and looked straight at him. "What the hell are you doing?" I managed to grab his left arm to keep him in the passenger's seat. He just smiled at me with amusement and said, "It's really pretty out there don't you think?" He had a glint in his eyes and a smile on his face that showed so much peace. The San Francisco Bay was glistening and mirror-like. The buzz of humanity was quieter than normal, or was that how I perceived it? There was a moment of stillness in which I caught my breath and just glanced at him, maintaining the car in its lane on the Bay Bridge.

"Honey, you are frightening me!" I said. "You are scaring me. Do you think you made the wrong decision? We can turn around and go back to the radiologist and tell him you want the treatments." I was panicking and still driving, keeping my fear in check since he resisted the temptation to step out of the moving vehicle on the bridge. He shut the door.

He smiled at me again and said in a very small voice, almost boy-like, "I'm sorry I scared you, but I have made a decision and I want to go like my mom did." I knew he was again lucid.

Larry had watched his mom die just five months earlier at the family cattle ranch in northern California. She had been diagnosed with lung cancer just around Christmas, did the radiology, and tried one dose of the chemotherapy, which would have killed her immediately if she had continued. She told her children and husband, "Just take me home. That's where I want to live out my life." They did. They honored her wishes, and she was gone within two months. Larry watched his dear mother go through the multitude of doctors and too-late treatments. He helped support his sisters and dad as they monitored and tended to his mother's needs. It was personal for his mom. The home that her husband had built for her when they wed fifty-eight years earlier was where she was most comfortable. This was where she wanted to leave earth.

I managed to get back to my sister's place. It was blazing hot outside. She had a small single-wide trailer in a trailer park in Pleasant Hill. It was fixed up nicely on the inside—it was her getaway and her sanctuary to get her closer to her job in San Francisco. Mounted at her sliding glass door entrance was a plaque that said, "Habitat for Her Sanity." A phrase that was so appropriate for what I was going through at the moment. She would go home to her husband in Turlock after putting in a three- or four-day workweek in San Francisco. She was out of town at the time and graciously offered it as a temporary place for us to use until we got a place to live. I didn't know how long the process was going to take and when (or if) I would have him lucid again. He was definitely in his own happy world. And even though the air conditioning was working, it was still sizzling hot in that metal trailer!

I called hospice later in the afternoon. I felt drained from the drive, my energy just sapped from the last twenty-one days of fear, making decisions, trying to reason out what was happening. Hospice sent over a notary that night for him to sign documents. He was lucid and understood the living will implications. The notary came with papers that would help with the process of using hospice services and signed the document, making sure his decision to die this way was what he wanted. The hospice workers comforted me. They sent a nurse the next day with medications that would calm him down—morphine and other liquid medicines to make him feel less restless, to quiet him down. The care package also had bed napkins and Depends. Why wasn't there Xanax or something else for me?

Oh, he was so restless. He would stand in his "Parkinson's stance" and freeze, his legs locked up. But then he would find movement and just wander around, taking things apart. A couple of times, he took my sister's phone apart. He went to the bathroom, came out, handed me a part, and said, "Here, I don't know how it came apart, but it was interesting." His face had the look of a young toddler looking for things to touch.

One of those nights up at our ranch house, he went to the bathroom and fell. He tried to catch himself and used the toilet roll holder as a handle. Upon his fall between the wall and the toilet, he created a big hole in the drywall where the holder used to be. It took all my strength to get him up from that position and back into our bed. I knew that night that we were in for a long struggle unless I sought help.

I was following after him like I would a toddler, hoping he wouldn't take anything else apart. He pulled the pin out on the fire extinguisher. He grinned at me when I said, "Larry, what am I going to do with you? You're breaking everything!" I was exhausted because this behavior had been going on for about three weeks and was getting more and more intense as the tumor grew. It was a very fast-growing tumor. Just by watching his face, I could tell that he really was in his own dream world, happy and relaxed, managing his impending death quite well. He didn't mind that he was locked in a Parkinson's stance and unable to move his feet. When he finally did move, he would topple and fall over into things.

I couldn't sleep that last night. I worried that if I dozed off, he would walk out of the place and into the street. He wouldn't sleep. When we were in bed together, I wrapped my arm and leg over him to hold him down and to calm him. He would get up, fall, and then I would have to pick him up off the floor, clean up the urine, try to get him back into one of those diapers, and calm him down again.

One of the times I picked him up off the floor; he became lucid and said, "I'm so sorry that I'm putting you through this, love."

I was hugging him tightly, standing there in the dark. He grabbed my face, pulled it away from his shoulder, and looked deeply into my eyes. He started kissing me passionately, loving me in a way he had not done in years. It was to be our last lovers' kiss. I stood by my husband, weak and confused—was this truly him? Or was his body going through medicine withdrawals? Those horrible medicines had taken away any possibility for lovemaking for years. I took what I could from that kiss and regret not acting on the opportunity to make it the last lovemaking we would ever have.

He had been taking many types of medications for years. First he took one for high blood pressure, and then the doctor said, "Let's give you medicine for your cholesterol." Combined with his Parkinson's medications that kept him moving in his "off" times, it was difficult to monitor the situation. There were also depression medicines and the anxiety medicines he had started taking years before to help him cope with his disease and loss of work. Thank God *my* depression medicine was working! I don't think I could have managed without Prozac.

The desire to care for my lovely husband took priority over caring for myself. I had to do that. What did I have to lose? Much! I loved him so much. Once we stopped all of his other medications and just used the ones the hospice sent to help him with restlessness, things changed in him. He just wasn't there. He let go of all fear and awaited the results of the inevitable ... to move on to the end of his life. He did it willingly, without pain, with much love.

The pain—the silent, gut-wrenching cry exploding from my heart. *How can I ever have the love I had again?*

> *Death is no more than passing from one room into another. But there's a difference for me, you know. Because in that other room I shall be able to see.* —**Helen Keller**

CHAPTER 3

A Fish Out of Water

When Larry left this world, I didn't know where I was going to go or what I would do. I had made a quick decision with the help of my daughter to get an apartment in the Bay Area, far and away from the house we had built five years prior in northern California. Hospice moved in the bed, but he never slept in it. Death was that quick.

We had an impromptu memorial at my daughter's house. You see, Larry had announced that he was an atheist at the age of nineteen and had never had patience with organized religion. No funerals, please! He and his mother had avowed years before that they both detested organized religion. So, the whole family—cousins and aunts, all thirty of them—came over and spread pictures all over the pool table. People came and went. We had his favorite food, Mexican, and his favorite dessert, Boston cream pie. My kids didn't miss a beat. They stood there for me, supporting me in my widow stupor. I felt like I was walking around in a dream that day.

Those who knew him least were polite and honored my children and me by their attendance. Those who knew him best showed up in the blue pocket T-shirts he always wore. He had about eight of them in his closet. He had such a quick wit and sense of humor that those moments were best presented, not talked about. That was him—quiet, reserved, polite, nonjudgmental to most, and above all, the best thing that ever came into my life.

The crying, the loneliness—no one to cling to, no one to return the emotion of love, to respect and witness.

The Monday following his death, my daughter took me to the Claremont Hotel for a day of pampering. It was so nice to feel the touch of a massage, the bubbling of the hot tub, and the deluge of the shower. I felt as if I was being cleansed of the all the emotions and grief that I had been silently swallowing to keep myself in check. On Tuesday, my son took me to do some wine tasting in Livermore Valley. Larry and I had always loved to do that in the Napa and Sonoma Valleys. On the fourth day, which would have been our thirty-sixth wedding anniversary, my daughter popped in and brought two dozen red roses and a card. She said that her daddy had asked her to do this for him; he had even signed the card in his Parkinson's handwriting. It was very small and barely legible, but it was there—"love Larry," in his own shaky handwriting.

One month later, well into the looming stages of grieving, I went through two weeks of crying, lying in my bed, huddled under the sheet. My respect for my mother increased twofold. She had gone through this. She was my role model, an example of how to live on without a partner. I surmised, *I will do that too!*

I had the strength of attentive friends who went with me on

a long-planned trip to Kauai, without him, with my sister-in-law in his place. He and I had never gone to Hawaii before and had planned the trip seven months prior to his diagnosis. With encouragement from my family and friends, I went anyway. The irony was that my name wasn't on the flight roster; *his* name was, both ways. My sister-in-law, always quick with the wit that emanates throughout his family, told me, "He's just reminding you that he really didn't want to go to Hawaii!" She was so right; he had never wanted to go there. It was never on our list of things to do. I had planned it to try to make his life better and more fun—or did I do it for me?

We had traveled some in the past decade, mostly to Europe. The Parkinson's disease that wracked his body left him without strength. We managed one big trip to Greece and Turkey on a cruise in the Eastern Mediterranean Ocean. By the time the flights were over and we arrived in Istanbul, he was pale and exhausted. He had gone on the trip because of me. He loved me enough to go with me on my long-desired "I've got to see Greece before I die!" trip. That had been a dream of mine since I was a child. I had read Mary Stewart's *The Moonspinners* at least four times, saw the movie just as many times, and fell madly in love with the Isle of Crete and the characters. Funny, our trip never took us to Crete. I know that it taxed him. I, the avid traveler, looked at it as excitement. He had never liked to travel far but was always game for adventure so long as I did all the planning.

I reminded myself that he wasn't a failure because he lacked enthusiasm for travel. It was his destiny that this happened to him. If he had been healthy, he probably would have loved to travel more. If I could have just kept him strong and healthy, then maybe our lives together would have been longer. Together we tried to make it better. It just didn't work out that way.

One of those nights in Kauai, I sat on the patio of my friend's time share, sucking in the ocean air and wavering from the large amount of wine that I had been drinking with my friends. They had long before gone on to bed. As I breathed in deeply, the grief just hit me horribly. I muffled my loud cries in my hands, convulsing as the grief pain flowed through my body.

The numbing effect of drinking increased the emotion of my ego. It reminded me that my life was really so sweet and full. Then, it felt empty like my wine glass. *Have some more ...*

Where can I go from here? I thought. *What is going to happen to me?* I cried into my hands. I tormented myself with a good thirty minutes of painful, wracking crying. Then I took a deep, sobbing breath and concluded that it was part of the process. I would be just like my mother and live twenty years alone, as she had after my father died. She was stalwart but plagued with bad health, and she kept a very healthy, positive disposition until her last fighting breath.

I reflected on my mother's death six years before, hearing the "death rattle" of her breath, in and out, in and out. Her health had always been horrible; she suffered from rheumatoid arthritis, fighting it for years. After three and a half years in a convalescent hospital, ending up with a prominent bedsore and paper-thin skin that would break if touched, she got meningitis and died. It was another death experience, another soul escaping to her source, happy to be out of that painful life experience. I endured. That's what you do.

I had seen and watched death early in my life. When my

grandmother choked on a piece of meat at our supper table when I was eighteen, my father tried to revive her. Nothing. Her body lay on the floor in our kitchen. My mother was in hysterics in the living room; my father went out in the driveway with the coroner. I started cleaning up the mess on the kitchen table, in a daze. I stepped over my grandmother's body and then looked down, got on my hands and knees by her, and cleaned up the defecation from her bowels that was on the floor—the last rites of what the body does when it gives up its soul.

There is never dignity in the body with dying. At the time, I thought that it was a humiliating experience, a lesson in how death can embarrass us when we are gone. Cleaning up was the honorable thing to do; I did not want my grandmother embarrassed. So I mustered the strength to follow through when others around me fell apart. Why is that?

A lot of things came to me on that trip to Kauai. The beauty of the island was really dimmed by Larry's recent death, my wonderful lover, my husband. I knew that when I got back to the mainland I would have to scope out a plan for myself, which I had always done so well for both of us. Now I had to do it just for myself. *How do I get from here to there?* I wondered. I started to look inward and reflect on the knowledge that I was of strong character and that this was just another bump in my path to wherever. I sensed this. I knew this.

> ***This fish was flapping and gasping for air.***

CHAPTER 4

Children ... Bless Them

When my son called me and asked me to attend the birth of his first child six weeks after Larry had died, I felt great anxiety. Thank God for the Prozac. Here was a momentous occasion for my son, and he couldn't share it with his dad. How could I be both parents at once? I replaced myself and pretended I was him. I knew that my son wanted to impress his Dad—I believed that *that* was what my son wanted—so I was my husband, not myself. It was a day of such mixed emotions, so much pain at not sharing this moment, and trying to control my inward crying over missing him so much.

When my son asked me to come into the delivery room to see his beautiful daughter, now *our* beautiful granddaughter, the tears in my eyes were almost relentless. They wanted to spill over (as they are when I type this), washing the pain of his absence away.

My life witness is gone. He vaporized in heavy breathing. The air

*was still and static with his last breath. How dare he leave me with such
emptiness?*

Our daughter had presented us with our first granddaughter
eight years before. I was there holding my daughter's legs open
as she was bearing down with all her might, and her estranged
husband was on the other side, telling her to push. How much I
wanted to slap him, the father of my soon-to-be granddaughter,
for hurting my dear daughter, for being the ass that he was.

It was so different for her than it was for me. I had a loving
husband by my side…there, by me, coaching me and loving me
when we gave birth to both of our children. She had a husband
with idle ways and a wandering heart…but who was there for the
birth of their child, because "he felt an obligation". He no longer
lived with her but was there for the blessed event. After all, this
was "their" first child.

As a mother to this beautiful daughter, I tried to accept the
fact that life is so different now for couples, including the process
of finding a life partner. We had simpler ideals and more of a
standard when I was young. It was very simple—work hard
together, don't expect too much from the other, and be partners.
Celebrate your successes; embrace the difficulties. Through thick
and thin. Sickness and health. *Yeah, right.*

We knew through our parents' example that a commitment
meant we would be with each other forever. Some of our friends
didn't make it; we did. We had respect for each other. We had love
and safety. We followed all the rules, including in our lovemaking.
We were young when we got married, neither experienced with
carnal issues. We grew up together when it came to sex. We
followed the rules: no cheating, be communicative (after thirty

years, this can get old!), always respect the inviolability of your partner, and accept and *respect* the differences. But at all times, be considerate of each other and have patience.

After my first granddaughter was born, Larry and I took care of her on weekends as my daughter struggled to support herself in a booming real estate market. My granddaughter and I bonded. I looked forward to those Sundays when she was with us. There were no issues; we stepped in when asked and willingly accepted. I always called it "Haley time." When the stresses of dealing with an ailing husband, working at a demanding job, and being the dutiful daughter to a convalescing mother would get to me, I'd call my daughter and say, "I need to be with her now to get my baby fix." She put me into a mode of positive feelings—all babies do. My daughter would say, "Come on over, Mom. She's all yours."

I lost my job, one that I had worked so hard at and was so proud of. It was the one good distraction that could remove me from dealing with Larry's health and the responsibility of caring for my mother. It was the one thing that I had that was my own and my security. It was the only salary that was paying the bills. We decided that we just needed to sell our house and move up into northern California.

We knew that the distance would remove us from our kids, but that's okay. They were adults and making decisions for themselves. This was *our* time, what time we had left together. We were forced into an early life of retirement with little funds. I was too young to collect retirement, and his disability would only pay the bills. We managed; we survived. We still had each other. This was our children's time too. We had raised them into successful, tax-paying citizens. We used to congratulate ourselves for that, all the time.

The children, so beautiful, cherished, innocent, and powerful. They are powerful with their instinctive knowledge that life around them is a gorgeous, sustaining lily pad to light on. Their chubby cheeks, their shiny eyes, their giggles in response to the silly adults making the silly faces. What power they have on us to put us into euphoria.

CHAPTER 5

The Finding of One's Soul

It had been over two years since his death. I was now living in a house I had bought in the Bay Area. I could buy a house for the same cost of renting an apartment; it just made sense. I was "balancing my books," trying to center myself. And at the moment, I was sitting at my computer, reading the e-mail messages from my son and my daughter:

The e-mail from son read as follows:

> Excuse me? Are you serious!? No discussion, you are just going to do what you want? I cannot believe you. It's your ball and you'll play it how you want, is that right?
>
> Just who do you think will rent a house out in the middle of nowhere? Do you think it'll be some quiet family that will take sweet care of the house? HA! Whatever they say the house will be trashed, damaged, and in no way livable when they're done.

If you are so hard up for money, why not offer to sell it to Grandpa? Ha! Are you doing this to support your going-out party life, paying Chris's way through life? Enjoy your fabulous cruise to Australia while some country bumpkin trashes your house!

And don't tell me Emily has done this before. She rents houses in towns, probably to people who have jobs and a reason to need to keep a place looking nice. Do you think you'll get the same type of renter on the ranch? Keep dreaming. Mom, this makes me sick at the thought that the house you and dad built together will be trashed because you need to save a couple of bucks makes me sick.

So fine, go ahead and do this with "no discussion" but you are way wrong. You are way way wrong in this and I cannot stand who you have become these last few years.

My daughter's e-mail read this way:

Hello Mom

It saddens me that we as a family cannot meet and discuss our issues in person. We all agree to disagree, however at the end of the day we need to find a resolution to this mess. Here are my issues …

1) The post office is our Heritage and should have never been put up for sale or a loan taken out on it. This is a debt that has been incurred for no reason. I know mom you stated the money was needed for buying the Bay Area house which is now an "asset" but this was also income that could have been used

to cover your expenses on the ranch house, hence we wouldn't be in this situation.

2) You stated several times the expenses incurred on the Ranch House, and many times I have offered to help. We even offered you cattle money to help and you stated "no thanks." When we spoke yesterday you said it costs you $300 a month out of pocket, and now from reading e-mails it is more? I would like to sit down and review these expenses so I understand more.

3) I do not want the Ranch house rented. This again is our Heritage, and feel by doing this you are creating more problems. Mom I have owned several rentals and know the wear and tear on a home it can cause. If this is happening why can't Dan and I meet the tenants and make the final decision? Also why are you using your niece and not a licensed real estate agent? I want confirmation there will not be any government assistance paying any rent.

I know once your mind is set, you do not change it. But I do promise you this my decisions are not based on GRIEVING or INHERITANCE as you stated in previous e-mails it is based on MORALS. Dig deep down inside mom and really think about these decisions you are making and are they morally right? When we discussed this a few weeks ago at the restaurant, I stated morals to you then and you said I was threatening you. Honestly, are you willing to continue to make these decisions based on money and lose your children and grandchildren? Mom please really think hard and reconsider this.

I love you ...

I didn't reply. It was too horrible of a time to receive this from my children. My kids were using emotional blackmail, threatening to remove me from their lives, because of a decision I had made regarding my resources that did not involve them in any way.

Two days later, I received a phone call from my daughter. I dreaded what was going to be said, knowing that the call was not going to be pleasant.

"Mom, how are you doing?" I could hear the anticipation in her voice.

I said in a calm voice: "Hi, sweetie. Are you back from Wisconsin?" I was trying hard not to think of the horrible e-mail she had sent.

"Yes, Mom, I got back yesterday. I got a series of e-mails from Dan, and you didn't respond to mine. Why aren't you answering it?"

I brought a computer into our household and showed them how to use it—and this was my payback!

"Well, I really have nothing to say. Your e-mail was clear, and we have a difference of opinion on what I am choosing to do with my life. Everything seems to be in the e-mails."

From there, the conversation went downhill. She got upset and told me, "You have changed. You are not the same mother I had five years ago. I feel that I have lost my mother too! It seems that all you have to say is 'me, me, me.'"

I interrupted her to say in a calm voice, "Isn't that what this call is all about? Isn't it really all about me?"

After a long, drawn-out, dramatic interlude, she finally said, "Well, if this is all the discussion that you want to have, to *not* include your children in decisions that you make, then you have another thing coming. I *will* put a lien on the house, you will not be able to rent it, and you will be alienated from the family."

The dialogue was exactly like that—at least, that is how I interpreted it in my emotional state, trying to hold onto my dignity. She continued her rant and then said, "I hope you have a nice life. I'm going to hang up now because you aren't listening to me. Good-bye. I love you."

I was numb to this reaction. This type of interaction between my daughter and me had been happening for over a year. Our relationship has always been more dramatic than most. I would like to say it's more her, and most people would agree with me, but my daughter, as smart and as beautiful as she is, does have a tendency to belittle those she loves the most (so I'd like to believe). I'd like to say that it is the result of grief over a changed mother, a mother who has shifted, a mother who has taken control of her life, found some bit of happiness, found herself attracting men in life, learned to love herself more, and found spirituality and a sense of being. Change is difficult to accept, and even adult children, like young children, don't like to see their parents change from the comfortable arena they were used to seeing them in. Parents are not supposed to have a life; they're supposed to just be there when *they* want them to be there.

Like the pupa exploding into a magnificent butterfly. How did I get here from there?

My mind then went back twenty-six months to the Christmas immediately after my husband's death. My daughter gave me a Christmas present of "sexy clothing and jewelry," including hoop earrings, a green satin blouse, sexy panties, and clothes that made me feel uncomfortable. It was all made for sixteen-year-olds.

It seemed to me that she was telling me I wasn't presentable—probably a very wrong interpretation, but my self-confidence was so low that I felt anything directed at me was a judgment. She said she wanted me to go out, to have fun! All right, she was right that I really wasn't presentable for a social life. But what would it take to change? I had never been the out-and-carousing party animal that she seemed to suggest I become.

My sensitivities were still on alert that Christmas. My grief over my loss would quicken rapidly. Someone in my family would crack a joke to try to lighten the mood, and I would go into overdrive. I would take offense at the innocent remark and run to the bedroom, hop into the bed, cover myself, and just take deep breaths. That's the only way I could handle the holiday then.

In February, on my fifty-seventh birthday, my daughter sent me to a weekend workshop in Nevada as a gift. It reminded me of the Erhard Seminars Training, or EST, that was so prominent in the mid-seventies. She had been encouraging me to go for a couple of years because she had taken several of their classes and felt they "opened" her up. "Mom, it is so helpful. It put everything in perspective for me. I know you will benefit." (Where were those lessons she had learned *now?*)

I hesitated several times. After my husband passed away—it had been a few months at this point—it seemed I had nothing else to lose. I told my daughter about my hesitation and that I didn't want to disappoint her. I said that I had been to many, many team workshops during my careers and political life, and they were beneficial at that time. I felt this one was geared only toward working people, and I just couldn't get my head into working right then. I went. I participated. It was intense.

There was one particular breakout session that may have kicked me into gear, a practice in which a little circle of people congregates as a group (there were twenty of us). Soft music was playing, the lights were lowered, and the instructor told us how to cultivate and nurture others with long hugs. We were separated into A and B groups. The instructor said that Group A would receive hugs and Group B would give them, adding that the giver should just nourish the receiver with a long hug. The receiver should not respond but hold his or her arms straight down. After about a minute, the instructor would say "A's, switch to another B, one that you have not hugged yet." This went on.

Each time I was held, I felt a terrible pull at my heart. When was the last time I had received such a hug, even just a touch? It had been many, many months, maybe even a year! Each person was different, male or female. The women were warmer with their hugs. Most of the men held back a little, except for one. Each was either uncomfortable in giving the hug or really into giving those hugs. When the fifth "A" put his arms around me, he was so calming, so considerate, and so warm. I melted. I was holding my arms as straight as possible, and the tears were running down my cheeks. I was holding back the emotions of months and years of having no outlet for my feelings related to all of my responsibilities, of not being nourished myself, of avoiding emotion. I tried to regain my composure.

After the exercise, the instructor had us all sit as he proceeded to tell a story. He started relaying a sad story about a person who had survived cancer. *Oh, great,* I thought. *This ought to help.* I was at the edge of a breakdown that I had resisted having since the day my father died. I starting weeping so hard that it shook every participant in the room to the bone. I convulsed and couldn't even recognize my own voice. Those sounds were coming from me! One participant came running across the room to me and took me in his arms. He calmed me and ran his hands through my hair as I was falling apart. I was saying to myself loudly, "Why didn't I make love to him? Why did he leave me this way? Why am I so sad?" It was a major pitiful display of the emotions I had pent up for over a decade. Oh, stalwart I!

On the last day, our graduation test required each participant to recite and yell as loudly as possible "The Star-Spangled Banner," a song most of us Americans grew up with. Some of the workshop attendees were from Canada and really had to concentrate on those words. Yelling at the top of my lungs across a room with an audience was one of the most significant memories of that weekend, other than the blasted crying the night before. But the good news is that I passed with flying colors and didn't have to repeat the test. Those who weren't familiar with the song had to sing it again and again until they passed it.

One of those amazing people was a Spanish speaker. He was a gardener for a landscaping business, but his employer had enough faith in his ability to go through this serious and emotional weekend in order to accumulate appreciation for himself. All of us were encouraging him over and over as he would stop and misstate the English words, which required you to start all over again. We were yelling at him and supporting him and shouting to him, "You can do this Juan! Put your heart into it!" He did, his emotional state was probably greater than mine...because of his inability to understand the words to the song. After the 5th time, one of the instructors asked him, "Juan, do you think you could sing this at the top of your lungs in Spanish?" Juan smiled back at him and said "Si". I never head the Star Spangled Banner sung so well in Spanish! He did it with such pride and perfection that it humbled us.

At the end of the weekend, with a busted capillary that made my left eye as red as if I had pink eye, I came away with a list of words that I had written on a board that I had broken in half with my hand, like with a karate chop. On one side, I had written "lack of purpose" on it. On the other side I had written these words: happiness, success, wealth, love, self-esteem, confidence, self-actualization, and La Vita de Loca. These handwritten words were intended to remind me of where I was and to push me to become a happier person. I still have that board. I still look at the list daily. It was a start for my self-inquiry.

Was it saving my soul or just saving my hide? My decisions ultimately were to become an independent woman not relying on anyone to help me. I never had that advantage of someone else doing the responsible thing. It was always I who provided the nourishment—the daughter, the wife, the mother. I knew that my strength was from within, and I was doing best what I thought would be good for me. No one else, just me.

The fluttering butterfly was searching for a place to land ...

CHAPTER 6

Saying Good-Bye

When I picked up Larry's ashes from the Neptune Society, I put them in my ranch house, not the apartment that I had rented. My children and I had decided that we would have a memorial—immediate family only—on his birthday, or near it at the end of April. I went up to the ranch house a few weeks before, planning for the small event. I felt lonely stepping into the house that he and I had built. This was our retirement home. It was beautiful in its setting out in a remote part of southern Humboldt County. It was a place that I could find peace and quiet, but it would also bring loneliness.

Everything that we did to the house, we did ourselves. It was difficult to find people with skills, and my Larry, who was so talented, was my fix-it man. I stepped into my front garden and looked at all the weeds that had grown from the wintery rain. They were everywhere! I started pulling. I turned my loneliness into anger and ripped and pulled for days. My arms hurt; my carpal-tunnel swelled in both wrists.

I took a couple of days off from all of the outside work and looked around the inside of the house. There was that hole in our bathroom wall that had to be mended. Every time I went up there since his death, I would look at that hole. It was a grave reminder of a serious dent in my life, a scar on my heart. And it reminded me that I no longer had a fix-it man around. The memory of how the toilet paper holder had broken and how he had fallen along the wall came flooding back to me every time I looked at it. The hole in the drywall was about six inches wide; sometimes I felt the hole in my heart was that big.

As I looked at the hole, I told myself, "*You* can fix this yourself!" With great intentions, I started the process. Of course, that meant I had to insert a screen, repair the drywall with plaster, and repaint the wall. At the end of the day, with a great sense of accomplishment, I opened a bottle of wine, poured myself a glass, and went out on my expansive deck to sip away. Acknowledging that I could most certainly do some things that he had done, I decided to change things up a bit in the house. I moved furniture. I scrubbed floors. I painted fences. I even power-washed the huge deck. Everything had to look perfect for this event.

By the time my children arrived for the memorial, my hands were thoroughly locked up and hurting tremendously. I didn't care. We needed to do this memorial to lay to rest an unfinished part of Larry ... and his ashes.

I had burned an audio disk of songs that he thoroughly enjoyed, funny songs and a few tearjerkers. I purchased a customized granite bench and put it on the ranch in a spot where he and I used to ride our four-wheeler to. It overlooked the Eel River above the old railroad tracks. We had made love there at one time many decades ago, and he used to hunt for deer there as a kid. This is the nature in which he grew up, and he cherished this place privately.

His sisters, his dad, and their children and grandchildren joined us for a picnic. The weather was so absolutely beautiful; the universe just presented an ideal moment for all of us. The music that played as we scattered his ashes across the field below the bench was "You Are the Wind beneath My Wings." I don't think anyone paid attention to that detail, but as I reflect on the pictures that we took that day, I notice that my children, their spouses, my granddaughters (one was only eight months old), and the rest of the family were smiling and enjoying themselves. But he truly was the wind beneath my wings.

The next day, my children left to go back to their respective jobs and homes, and I finished up my small chores and left. I felt like I had accomplished a great deal, physically and mentally.

If I had a single flower for every time I think
about you, I could walk forever in my garden.
—Attributed to Claudia Ghandi

CHAPTER 7

Stepping Out

Driving back down Highway 101 from that memorial weekend, I mentally worked out a process to move on because I truly needed to. When I got home to the apartment and got the cats out of the car (throw up and all!), I earnestly jotted down a list. Priority one—take care of myself and get healthy. Over all those years of caregiving, I had become many pounds overweight. It was easier to eat my feelings, and I did a great job of it. It didn't hurt that I had a husband who loved to cook and enjoyed my cooking as well.

I immediately signed up at a gym and started working out. I joined Jenny Craig and started a regimen of diet and exercise. I also signed up on one of those Internet sites to see if there was a possibility for me in the love area. After all, it was one of those words on my board, right? I tried Match.com. It was free, so I really didn't have anything to lose, right? When I signed up, meandering through the site with trepidation, I started to reach out. After all, they couldn't see me, could they? I created a profile that I thought would represent me. When it asked for marital status—single, divorced, separated, or widowed—I checked the "widowed" box, feeling a pang. Just using the word *widow* seemed so desperate and lonely. Surprisingly, I got a hit within a day! I started corresponding with a guy who was about five years younger than me. When he started calling me, I was so flattered.

There were so many possibilities here. *Could there be another life for me?* I wondered. I was exhilarated that someone would even be interested in me. Could I live up to the expectations of a single life that I had never really experienced? He lived in the same town as I did. He was a professional, primarily in the same field I had worked in for so many years. We connected. He would call each afternoon, and we would talk and talk and talk. He was seducing me with promises that once he got off his night-shift work, we would meet face to face.

He would call, and I would put on background music. His sweet-talking self would make me promises of dancing and romance. I even promised him that when we met, I'd bring him homemade brownies, which he said that he adored. He complimented me more.

I would go to the gym daily and work out on the machines, watching those cute, young guys in front of me. What a distraction! The thought that I could think that freely seemed to warm my senses and arouse my sexuality. Was I still alive that way? Could I be loved by someone again?

Michael continued to call with promises of meeting me. This dragged on for weeks. At one point, he stopped calling. He finally called me one more time, and I told him that I believed it was time for us to meet. He anguished about that because of his heavy work schedule. He finally relented and said yes, and then we agreed to meet at a local restaurant at noon on Cinco de Mayo. Of course, I picked a Mexican restaurant.

I was excited. I had my nails done, got a pedicure, waxed those eyebrows, and got a haircut. I even waxed those "nether regions" that hadn't been touched in years. Never had I done that before! *I can dream, right?* I thought. I carefully picked out an outfit that was flattering. I had to buy smaller clothes because my gym visits were pushing my body into a slimmer form. I had energy, and I felt marvelous!!!

The day arrived. I carefully dressed and put on my makeup. The butterflies were in my stomach, something I hadn't felt in a long time. I knew what he looked like and he me; we had pictures on our Internet profiles. I felt an exuberance in me that said, *Wow, you look awesome!* Lots of positive self-talk got me out of that car and across that parking lot. *You are beautiful. You are an accomplished woman* … I was doing that internal talk that really boosted my self-confidence. It cooled the fear that this meeting could end up as a failure.

Walking from the car through the busy parking lot, my self-doubt was saying, *He's probably sitting in his car watching you to see if he wants to walk into the restaurant.* I may have been right.

I walked with purpose and a bounce. *Hey, did I notice those men turn around and glance at me when I walked by them?* Maybe it was just my imagination.

I went into the restaurant, and the hostess asked me if I wanted to sit. I told her I was meeting someone there and looked around her toward the bar. Nope, not there. I asked to walk into the dining room. Nope, not there either.

We were supposed to meet at 1:30, and it was 1:35. *Okay, so he got called into work,* I reasoned. He said that if he got called in, he would call me. I told him that I would wait for him only thirty minutes; after that, it was "sayonara." I meant it. I waited. I checked my cell phone, just in case. I told the hostess that I would wait a few more minutes. I did wait. I called his cell and left a message—"Hey, Michael. I'm here at the restaurant, just wondering if you forgot we were going to meet or something serious came up. Please let me know. I'm waiting."

So I waited the whole thirty minutes and got a bit angry—okay, a lot angry. I left the restaurant and went back to my apartment, took off my clothes, got in my gym clothes, and immediately went to the gym. *Damn! Why are men so sly? Why are they so skittish?* All of these ideas were going through my head. Maybe he did see me from his car and decided to not join me. *Maybe. Probably. Very likely!* My doubts soared, and my self-esteem just plummeted.

Days went by. I continued my daily routine. Soon, my daughter called me. She knew about this Michael guy and that he and I were having some phone conversations. I tried to keep her informed on what her mom was doing. After all, it was she who gave me those hooker earrings and told me to go out, right? She asked me how things were, and I told her about the hoax date. She said, "Mom, don't you realize? He's married!" I paused. That had never crossed my mind. I naively assumed that if you put your name on a dating site, you were single. Boy, was I in for a surprise, and I learned a lesson to be cautious in this single/dating arena. I calmly said to her, "Can I see Haley? I need some Haley time."

Michael called a couple of weeks later. He meekly apologized for not showing up, saying that he had to work and that he had come down with a bad cold. I told him that I didn't think there was any possibility of a connection between us anymore and to have a nice life. *Wow! Did that come from me?*

My checklist needed updating: Married life – scored pretty much perfectly. Single life – *needs a lot of improvement.*

I decided that I would need to be cautious in the Internet dating arena and signed up with eHarmony.com, which has a subscription fee. I figured that maybe that site did better filtering of the candidates. After all, my son and his wife met that way. So I continued searching on the Internet. I searched many times on that site and could not find a single interesting person. Was this an omen? Would I be single for the rest of my life, like my mother? Months went by without a bite. I revamped my profile, taking away the checkmark by "widow", putting one by "single." At that defining moment, I knew that my life was moving forward. Maybe it was *me* moving forward?

> **Stepping out can wait for a while.**

CHAPTER 8

Catching My Breath

After Larry's death, the hospice organization told me that they offered many types of meetings and workshops for survivors. Going to them made sense to me because, somewhere, I could identify with a group of people who had gone through this painful part of life. I went into the room after introducing myself to the counselor and saw boxes of tissues on the tables around the room. The people were warm, but the mood was solemn. About fifteen people were in the room, and they all introduced themselves to me.

Politely, each person in the circle explained their circumstances. My introduction was, "Hi. My husband has been gone for four months, and I'm here to listen and see if I can get any solace from this group." Each person's story was different but the same. We had all lost someone in our lives. We all were shaken to the core. One man, so distraught in telling his story, broke down. The boxes of tissues were passed around. Another man was telling his story and said that his daughter was no longer talking to him. She was mad at him because he had finally gotten rid of his wife's piano. He explained that he had asked his daughter if she wanted it, but she said she didn't. He explained that he sold it to a young family looking for a piano, and they removed it from the house for him. His daughter became incensed that he had made such a move without discussing it with her.

One couple, I noticed, were holding hands. They introduced themselves as Carl and Lydia and said they had met in the group three years earlier, after each of them had lost a spouse. They were much younger than me, and they looked like they were in love. They affirmed my observation when they said that they were together and that it was because of the group that they had met and found each other. They came to the meetings for whatever reason, citing the camaraderie among the group members when explaining why they had been coming for over three years. *Over three years!* I thought. *Oh, my God. You've been coming here for three years and are still seeking solace?* My mind quickly jumped ahead, and I saw myself there, telling the old story. *Sorry, Larry*, I thought. *You and I talked about this before. Sweetie, I would never have wanted you to sulk around if I left this earth first, and you admitted to me that you would not want me to do this either.*

I never went back to that group. I believed that I was being empathetic, but I could not wrap my head around the idea that the grieving process could be so awful. I never went back. I was probably in denial.

I walked out of that room and took a big breath!

CHAPTER 9

Moving On

When I originally moved back down to the Bay Area after Larry passed away, I wasn't intending to stay there for long. I figured I'd be there about a year and then graciously move back to the ranch house, lick my wounds, and just be a nana with a house for grandchildren to visit. It was beautiful there. Peace was there. Memories were there.

But it was so far away from my kids, so far away from my granddaughters, who got me to my happy place.

While in the Bay Area, I managed to connect with businesswomen of like minds. I had a consulting business that I dabbled in and decided to become a member of the local chambers of commerce. I checked that off my list of things to do in order to move forward. I was very politically inclined and filed a DBA from the county. I became a member of the women's group and decided to focus on my business. That would take my mind off of the loneliness, I figured.

No hits on eHarmony … yet.

In May, I rejoined a women's organization called Soroptimist International. I had been an active member in the club up in Garberville. At the annual conference, one member and I were browsing the other club tables outside the meeting room and came across an announcement that the international conference was being held in Taiwan in July. We looked at the pamphlet. The trip was discounted, and the Summer Olympics were going to be in Beijing. We'd be there just before the Summer Olympics. Oh, my! An adventure! And traveling with a healthy person! We booked the trip.

So off I went to China for two weeks with my new friends. It was memorable. We had fun. We laughed, told jokes, and just enjoyed ourselves. I felt like my old self again. I went to Hong Kong, Beijing, X'ian, and Taiwan, each place different and exciting to explore. I had never in my life thought that I would travel to China. I bought so many souvenirs that I had to buy another small suitcase to pack them in.

At the end of the trip, when I got back to my apartment, my daughter and granddaughter had decorated it with a "Welcome back, Nana" banner and signs that said "We missed you!" Balloons and confetti were everywhere. It was truly sweet. My daughter was so comforting to me.

Finally home from China, I threw myself into my regimen of transformation. I went back to the gym and continued to lose weight. I was feeling great! I even decided to go to the Democratic convention with another group of female friends. I had previously tried to get a seat as a delegate, but those were sewn up by the local politicians in Alameda County. I had not had the time to make myself known to them so I could get the precious assignment. So in August, do or die, we were going to go. We volunteered and went to the convention in Denver. Oh, it was so much fun! We even decided that if the Democratic candidate won, our next big trip was going to be to Washington DC for the inauguration.

Along comes September. It had been over a year since Larry had gone. I had managed to transform myself a little. I went to a psychic with my daughter because it was deep inside of me, and her, that somehow, if we could make contact with Larry, we would feel better.

My daughter was going through some problems and needed some consolation. She had provided that for me, so I booked us flights to New York City. She had just ousted her second husband – a man with many bad childhood memories. He had lost his mother in a tragedy at the age of 14, a tumultuous age. When Larry died, it was his excuse to use for his own personal anguish. Sometimes all the counseling in the world can't help those who aren't ready to help themselves. My daughter, somehow she was a survivor. *It's definitely genetic.*

Earlier that year she had undergone a hysterectomy with no more chances of having any more children. She was down....so we went for a long weekend together. The hour we spent with a renowned psychic gave me pause. It validated an understanding of there being a single source--a source that we all know...but can't put our minds to because of our indoctrination to religion while growing up. In this reading, my husband came through.

This psychic knew only that we were from somewhere in California and that we were mother and daughter. He was accurate in his descriptions of those who came through—my uncle, my aunt, and my *mother*! Good grief! And my mother was playing cards! Yes, in her life here on earth, she loved card games. My siblings and I were raised by parents who taught us well. The card games stimulated our math skills and strategies, and humor was always part of us all.

The psychic stopped in his reading and told us, "I've never seen this before," and he chuckled. "There is a man," he said. "He is near your right shoulder. Is this your husband?" I confirmed that it probably was. The psychic continued, "He didn't believe in this channeling and metaphysical stuff, did he? He was cynical ... or skeptical?" I replied, "Probably both!" and I really couldn't help smiling. My daughter was just gleeful. She was just as happy as I was that someone was really in touch with our lost love.

He continued and said laughing, "He is in an I Dream of Jeannie outfit—purple, with one of those hats like Carnac the Magnificent from the Johnny Carson show." My daughter just burst out laughing and s*aid, "That sounds like my dad—always the humor and with sarcasm!" She was so right.* The psychic said, "He says that your wish is his command!" I knew Larry was letting us know it was truly him in his own way, a true skeptic even from beyond, and the reading continued.

I walked away from that reading with confirmation of a source. There is communication going on between our physical selves and those who have moved on. It is always happening. It is always there. I have always felt it there. I felt better when I got home. I felt that I had achieved a connection with my lost love that would settle my mind in terms of the loneliness that I was experiencing. I pulled out my old books of self-help and metaphysical teachings and proceeded to delve into this arena.

I was happier than I had been in a long time. It was time to move on.

So when I got home after my New York trip, it was time to get busy and get serious about having fun. I removed my profile from eHarmony; there wasn't any significant interest coming from it, and it was a waste of money. Friends had told me about a dance club nearby that attracted a lot of "older" singles. I talked about going but wasn't sure I could find the courage to walk in by myself. Being home every night alone was getting a bit overwhelming, and I knew I had to take matters in my own hands. I finally decided to give it a try.

The place was called Badabing's and was in San Ramon. My daughter said, "Mom, that's where all the cheaters go and dance with old people." I thought, *So, I'm old? Not on your life have you got me buried yet, baby.* That was probably the impetus behind going to the dance club. I walked into the darkness. Music was blaring over a large, wooden, well-varnished dance floor. Many people were dancing, and those who weren't were sipping on drinks. They weren't *old*! They all looked about my age. They were vibrant, they were smiling, and they looked happy!

So as I was standing there like a wallflower, I was thinking, *How does one get to dance? Do you ask the guys? Has socializing as a single woman changed enough that asking a guy would be inappropriate?* One guy did come up and asked me to dance (*WOW!* I thought. *Is it possible to attract another man in my life?*), and afterward he politely introduced himself. "Hi, I'm Ken," he said. "You're new here, aren't you? I'm a regular here, and I haven't seen you here before.

I told him that, yes, he was correct that I had never been

there before. We talked a bit, and I ended up telling him that I was new to the dance scene after being off the market for a long time. He said, "Oh, so you're recently divorced?" The very honest me had to curtail my answer to a simple, "No." Then he asked, "Separated?" I wasn't trying to be coy, but how do you just blurt out to some guy who you've just met, "No, he's dead." So I said, "No ..." and pointed to the ceiling. Would you believe that he looked up? Then he got a look on his face when he recognized what I really meant with that gesture, and he apologized. "Oh, I'm so sorry!" It was a hard story to follow with any conversation. He walked away and asked another lady to dance.

I stayed for a couple more hours. I just sat back near the wall and the large speakers and breathed in the energy of the people dancing on the floor, the music, and the vibrations from the speakers. I put my purse on my shoulder and walked out, feeling lighter than I had in months. I was definitely going to come back again.

One day, while I was driving on the freeway near my apartment, I saw a sign that read, "www.dublinsingles.com." I thought, *Why not? It's local. Try one more time?*

That Internet site led me to a place called Great Expectations. I remembered getting mail years before from that company. Even before it became an Internet dating service, Larry would receive the envelope at our house addressed to him directly. I would tease him and say, "Are you trying to tell me something?" He would just laugh and say, "I can't figure out why they have my address, but I'm sure if *your* name was on it, you'd be calling them!" So there I was fifteen years later looking for someone from the same company that he and I would tease each other about.

I called the phone number, fell for the whole sales pitch, and signed up. They took expensive photos and interviewed me, and I picked out a great video interview to post with my profile. The most difficult thing for me to do was decide on the wording for my profile. I had to revamp it several times before it finally said what I wanted it to say. I wanted to be upbeat, so I used this wording: "I have a positive outlook on life and know that it gets better and better each day. I am not shy and very adventuresome. I love to laugh and play. Can you make me laugh?"

It was early October, and within one week, I got my first e-mail of interest. His profile and video were interesting to me. His name was Ernie. While watching the video, I kept looking for any signs of dishonesty, but all I saw was a very honest and happy guy. So I sent him a message saying that I was interested. He was nice on the phone. He was a few years younger than me, had raised his son by himself, and lived just a few miles from me. We talked on the phone several times over the next couple of weeks.

A friend of mine who I had not talked to since Larry had died called me one day. She and I got together, and we decided to go up to the ranch house to have a "girls' weekend." We drank wine, talked, admired the beautiful view from my deck, and decided to talk about metaphysical life.

We had gone to a metaphysical-based store in Eureka and found a video called *The Secret Behind the Secret*. We popped it into the DVD player and had a marvelous time going over it. A couple years before, a popular book and movie called *The Secret* had been released. I loved the movie the book so much that I bought four of them and gave them to my son, daughter, and sister as gifts for Christmas. When my friend and I got back to the Bay

Area, we even signed up to attend a meet-up group on the laws of attraction.

She and I decided to go to a holistic fair that was being held close by, figuring we could amuse ourselves with the materials related to the occult and voodoo magic, which we were both prone to believe in. It was fun talking about these things with someone. At one booth, the people were selling audios for meditating. Since we had seen *The Secret Behind the Secret*, I had been trying to practice some form of meditation. It had been years since I had done that.

Little did I realize that I had been subconsciously meditating for years by putting on my soothing music. I used that method to prepare for the birth of my children, and it was so helpful. It did put me in a calm space. I took home the audio, listened to it, and was really happy with the purchase. It was definitely opening me up for my future. So when I got home that night, I revised my Internet profile to reflect my feelings:

> *I have a positive outlook on life and know that it gets better and better each day. I am not shy, and very adventuresome. I love to laugh and play. I also love my independence, my male friendships, and my open attitude toward life. And yes, I can be naughty!*

> *My life is unfiltered and without baggage. I like nature and quiet when it is needed, but can whip out fun and a quick remark better than most. I know there are more of you out there and would love to see if there is anyone out there who can challenge me. I am very romantic and sensual and truly love the things that women love ... BUT I also can give the same in return.*

My idea of a really good weekend is near the ocean with the waves romping at my toes. If you see the glass as half full then maybe we have a lot in common ... Seeking you in the universe, somewhere!

CHAPTER 10

The Dates

I again talked to Ernie on the phone, and he talked about his son soon going into the Navy and how he had parented him as a single dad. He told me that he had been single for over fifteen years, which he spent basically just working and raising his son. We talked some more. It didn't sound too promising to me, but he really was funny, just like I had asked. I got back onto the website and started reviewing the other single men near me and their videos.

Another one caught my eye. He talked about meditating, and that resonated with me. I sent him an e-mail saying that I was interested. The following day, I got a call, and it was from him. He spoke with a funny New York/Bronx accent and said he would like to meet with me, either that day (it was Friday) or Saturday. He asked why I had selected him, and I replied that I liked what he said about being quiet and meditating. He asked if I liked country music, and I told him that I hadn't really been out enjoying music lately, but that would be great. His name was Chris, and he said, "Good. Then why don't I meet you at the Clayton Saloon in Clayton?" My heart said, *Go for it!* so I told him I would meet him there at 9:00 p.m. It was 3:30 when we hung up the phone. Panic!

I kind of shrugged the panic off and gradually got myself ready. I was thinking about his accent, and it reminded me of the three years that Larry and I had lived in New York. It was a really memorable time; we were young and had no children. We had moved there on our own early-adult adventure. We were two California newlyweds who had just moved to New York so Larry could attend the Culinary Institute of America. We were so excited about that adventure. We made friends and experienced a culture different from that of our California upbringing.

When I drove up to the old saloon in my car, there was Chris, his body was parked on the bench in front of the saloon with his legs out-stretched, looking very comfortable in the landscape. He jumped up as he recognized me in my car and pointed to a place for me to park. His looks weren't a surprise; his profile and video were very accurate. He had this short shockingly white hair, which created a distinguished aura around him. He seemed really fun and had an energy surrounding him. He walked me into the saloon and we sat at the bar. He bought our drinks, and we started to talk. As soon as he captured the conversation, I was just amazed at the humor and fun that he was emanating.

Listening to him with his colorful language, I thought, *This could get interesting.* His crusty New York/Bronx accent was decorated with words like *fuck* and *goomba*. He also included words like *pussy*. I hadn't heard that one come from any man's mouth so casually. He told me jokes too (after all, I had put in my dating profile "Can you make me laugh?")

He explained that he had been in the Bay Area for about two years, having moved here from Las Vegas. He was a musician at heart, a professional drummer for almost fifty years. He informed me that his day job was working as a courier for a Berkeley law firm. He also told me that he loved Las Vegas because of the night life and the gigs he could pick up, but his other calling was his spirituality. His real family was in an ashram in Oakland.

Right there, I gained an education on what it means to be a Siddha Yogi. I just thought "yoga" was an exercise! My life expanded in this new knowledge of religions and spirituality. This was something that I had been missing for years.

While talking, he showed me his Bronx streak, with speech peppered with profanity, but then his passion for his spirituality came out. I commented, "It really sounds like both your passion for music and your passion for spirituality could have you dancing back and forth in almost a bipolar state." He looked at me a bit perplexed, trying to understand me. And he said, "All I want is to leave this body and be with my guru."

That statement shocked me at first. I barely understood what he was really communicating. Was he talking suicide? No, this wouldn't be correct. We continued to talk about meditation, which was a funny discussion to be having in a country bar. It just seemed so odd. I shared my story with him, and he seemed to have no empathy for the "poor widow," just a passing understanding of my loss. He continued to emanate from a very happy place. I asked him if he had lost anyone to death, and he explained that the closest loss was his ex-wife's mother. He commented that it had been over fifteen years ago. I think he recognized immediately that it was a heavy topic and switched to talking about his son.

He talked proudly about his twenty-three-year-old son who was attending Berklee College of Music in Boston, another drummer for the world. I said, "Well, looks like he had quite a role model," and Chris just beamed. He asked me to dance, and we really had great time on the small, wooden floor of the old saloon. I loved the country songs and the quaintness of the Clayton Club. I asked him what he was doing for Thanksgiving, and he explained that since he had no family here on the West Coast, he very likely would be eating at some friends' house or not at all.

He explained that his mother and father were both still alive and that his dad, who was close to ninety, still lived in the house where he had grown up in the Bronx. He said that he was thinking of going back there for a short time, just for a couple of days, for his dad's birthday in February, but he hadn't made up his mind yet about the travel. We had some really good laughs, and I told him that I hadn't laughed like that in a long time. I thanked him for it, and he said, "I'm just an artist, and I love it when others laugh at my presentation."

We went out behind the club, where the full November moon was lighting the sky in full regalia. The weather was unusually warm, almost summer like. There was sensuality in the wind. It was a gorgeous night to meet someone new. I felt a shift in my life then.

After that evening, Chris and I talked on the phone a couple of times, and I called my son, Dan, to ask if he minded if I brought a date to his wife's annual family Thanksgiving dinner. There were usually about sixty people there, and the year before had been my first time to go alone, without Larry. I really didn't want to go by myself. My daughter and her family would be there, but if Chris went with me, at least I would have someone to use as an excuse to leave without feeling obligated to stay. Dan called me back and said, "So long as you pay for his dinner, Mom, there would be no problem." I hung up and immediately called Chris.

I said to Chris, "My kids and granddaughters are going to this large Thanksgiving dinner. I really don't want to go but need to show my face. It would be great to have someone with me. I'll have to drive up to Sacramento, and it would be great to have company. My son said that I could bring a guest. Are you up for it?" He didn't hesitate, saying, "I would love to be with a large family since I'm missing mine. Thank you for inviting me."

> *Do not dwell in the past, do not dream of the future, concentrate the mind on the present moment.* —*Buddha*

CHAPTER 11

Thanksgiving 2008

That Thanksgiving morning, Chris drove over the hill from Oakland to my apartment in Dublin and then went with me to the Folsom restaurant. It was an enjoyable drive, during which we listened to his music and some of the music I had downloaded from the Internet that I thought might qualify as country. He was beating his hands on the dashboard to the beat of the music. His energy was amazing, and I started to feel really silly about being with him. He was so boyish for an almost-fifty-nine-year-old. I was feeling a sense of fun coming from this connection.

On our way to the dinner, he called his mother and father. As I listened to him speaking to them, his voice revealed the utmost love for his parents and that he truly missed being there in New York. He explained to them that he was going to be with his new friend and her family and was looking forward to a family get-together. When we showed up, his magnetism immediately radiated through the restaurant. He is just that kind of guy—an artist. My kids were meeting one of "Mom's dates" for the first time. A couple of times, he kissed me on the neck when he walked by me. So cool! An outward show of affection was something I had not experienced from a man ever. Public displays of affection were new to me. I could tell by the looks on my daughter and son's face that this might not have been a good idea. They showed hesitance with mild reactions. My son was truly engaging, being such a friendly person himself.

My daughter had her new boyfriend there also. She had been dating him for several months, and I had met him once before. She was flashing a diamond ring on her hand, which I had noticed but did not acknowledge. She had not even called me about it. I was way too distracted by the situation at hand. *Perhaps bringing Chris to this was wrong?* I thought. (I had doubts for many weeks afterward.)

He loved little children, and there were several of them around us. His personality was a bit rough around the edges. I wasn't used to someone so outgoing. He was Italian and raised in the Bronx, a true spirit from one of our nation's toughest cities. I focused on making sure nothing was said to upset anyone. He had a tendency to drop the F bomb casually in conversation, and he loved telling jokes that were off color. I felt like I was walking on eggshells. My daughter-in-law was hosting the event, and she took event planning very seriously. She had only been married to my son for two years and had just had a baby, so I was really alert about acknowledging her planning and purpose for this event. It was her family, not mine.

When we drove back to my apartment, he gave me a really nice kiss and said that he enjoyed being with my family and me. I told him that I really enjoyed the day.

The Friday after Thanksgiving, I got a call from Ernie. "Hi,

Lori," he said. "I was wondering what you might be doing today?" I told him that I wasn't planning anything, and he said, "Would you like to go miniature golfing with me today?" *Okay*, I thought, *why not?* I said, "It sounds like fun, and I've never been miniature golfing." Ernie said, "Then I'll come by and pick you up around two o'clock." I was game for anything. After all, I did sign up for a dating service, and if you ask for it, it will come, right? It seemed the laws of attraction were really at work.

Ernie drove up in this beat-up little car (signs of a long-time bachelor?). He was such a friendly guy, and we had an amazing time putting the colored golf balls around the miniature course. Ernie, a natural flirt, managed to get my attention a couple of times by hitting my ball off the course on purpose. This was cute, and I admit, I felt like I was sixteen years old again. The discussion of my widowhood came up, and I told him a little about my late husband.

He asked about his health, and I told him that after a prolonged case of Parkinson's, Larry had died of brain cancer. He said the appropriate, "I'm sorry." Then, to smoothly transition away from the subject of death, Ernie told me about his health. He was only fifty-two, but he had already had a heart attack. The minute he said those words, my mind went into overdrive:

Okay, Lori, you have already gone for a ride with a sick partner. Is this the one for you? I pondered this for a minute. *Not!* My mind was yelling at me. *So, when you date fellows over a certain age, statistics say that it's very likely they are going to be more unhealthy than you. Isn't that why women live longer than men? Geez, I just don't want to go down that road!* My mind was reeling with the possibilities. *Shift gears here, mind. This guy is really a nice man. Be a little open. Don't be so judgmental!*

When we were through with the course, we went to a quick-serve restaurant where you go to the counter and order, and then you sit there and eat. *Okay, so this isn't a real date.* He had coupons for the miniature golf and the food didn't come with candles—so what? Was my cynical mind really going to blow? I just couldn't figure it out. While we ate our Mexican (fresh) food, our topics went a bit off-kilter. It was just after the November election; my guy had won, and I was quite proud of that. We were fine until we started to discuss California Proposition 8, which was against same-sex marriage. He brought it up, and I'm no shrinking violet when it comes to civil rights, but I did aim high on my convictions. We more or less walked away disagreeing with each other's side of the argument.

So, he was a devout Christian and a Republican ... and me? Well, I was raised Protestant but not devout, and I hadn't thought twice about organized religion in many years. I was a Democrat and proudly so, and I told him that. Such a polite guy. He took me home.

The next day, he called me to reflect on our opposing positions, and he said, "I think we broke two of the major rules on a first date: one, you should never discuss politics, and the second one is never discuss religion."

I agreed with him and thanked him for the date. It would be many, many months before I heard from him again. That night, I reflected on the date and got a bit depressed, so I called Chris.

I asked him if he would go with me to Rodeo Beach the next day. I told him that I would gladly drive. I would pick him up at his place in Oakland, and he could join me in a memory visit to Fort Chronkite, the Army housing base where my family had lived when I was a child. It was just north of the Golden Gate Bridge, and I packed a picnic of "healthy" foods.

It was a gorgeous day and we hung out sitting on one of the benches. We hiked above the hills and I even pointed out one of the barracks I lived in as small child, and it was still there. It was a beach in Marin County. There were many people on the beach with their families enjoying this late November day. It was so clear and beautiful. We sat on a bench overlooking the beach and he grabbed my hand to hold it. My mind and memory reflected back to my high school years. What memories of walking on a beach in Mendocino, with a boyfriend and listening to the waves. This guy from the Bronx had no idea that I was a bit melancholy because of those memories.

The last time I had been to Rodeo Beach was with Larry, about twenty-eight years before. I shared that with Chris—I could tell that this was not his kind of date. We sat and held hands some more. We talked on the way back. It was a stilted discussion about nothing, really. I sensed in him that he was just humoring me and that he really didn't have anything else to say or do. When I dropped him off at his place back over the bridge, he kind of shrugged his shoulders and sauntered with his tough guy walk toward his place. He never looked back over his shoulder with any kind of expression, and I had a feeling I might not see him again.

When the world says, "Give up," Hope whispers, "Try it one more time."
                              —Author Unknown

CHAPTER 12

So, I Was Missing This?

It was early December, fifteen months since I had lost Larry. I really needed a good laugh after that trip to the beach. I was interested in going to the local comedy club for some laughter—and I really needed to do some good, *hard* laughing—so I thought, *What if I buy the tickets and ask him?* I called Chris one more time and told him, "Thank you for joining me at the beach last Saturday. I really appreciated that you came with me." He told me that he had enjoyed the day. He explained that he had gone to his ashram for meditation and went into detail about his guru and how it all really helps him become centered.

I said, "Chris, I really, really need to laugh, and I love being with you because you joke and it makes me feel better. Would you join me in going to a comedy club that is out here? I have the tickets and just need someone to go with me. Please do."

He said, "Sure, I'll meet you there, and we'll see what

evolves." *That was an interesting statement,* I thought. *What did that mean?*

It had been a long time since I had gotten my courage up to ask a man out for an actual date. *Wow! I've come a long way now!* When we met there, we had a great time. Since I had bought the tickets, he said that he would buy the drinks. There was a two drink minimum required. Because I was living a healthier life, I had stopped drinking most sugary drinks. I ordered a shot of tequila instead. He said that he normally didn't drink, but he ordered the same. He told me that the best high he'd had was from a shot of tequila, a beer, and then weed. He then proceeded to tell me about all the drugs he had taken much earlier in his life. I was thinking, *This man is so honest and frank that it can alarm someone if they don't get to know him better.* He talked about having those drugs around him all the time as a musician and how it seemed to be an accepted part of the business. But then he explained that he just can't treat his body that way anymore.

He said that he had brought with him a book of pictures of his family that he would love to share with me. I told him, "I would love to see them. Why don't you follow me home and you can share them with me there?" I felt a stir in my body in anticipation of what a third date could be like. *Is it appropriate? What would he expect?* All of these things were going through my mind. When I had been phone flirting with Michael (the loser), I had prepared for the eventful option that perhaps someone would find me appealing and want to make love to me. So I had stocked up with condoms and lubricants, necessities of today's dating singles.

When we got to my apartment, I introduced him to my cats.

He said in a very provocative way, "Oh, I love pussy!" I was thinking, *Uh-oh, am I prepared for this?* We sat down on my couch, and he showed me his family photos and some photos of him with Johnny Cash. That was impressive. I could tell the photo was over fifteen years old, but he was proud of his abilities as a musician, and I could tell that was very important to him.

I complimented him and told him how impressed I was with the pictures. He showed me photos of his mother and father, his son, and his ex-wife. He even brought a video taken of the three of them when they first moved to Oakland in the late 1980's.

He told me as he looked around my apartment, "You and your husband did everything right." I looked at him inquisitively. Then he said, "What you have here is really an abundance of comfort. My life has always been sparse. I have lived that way for so long. I never know where I'm going next."

I agreed with him there and said that I was thinking that I was feeling the same thing, asking myself, *Where am I going now?* I said, "Chris, when a couple is in a long-term marriage and did all the right things, that doesn't mean everything was done right. But I agree with you: *we* did things right, and he and I were able to enjoy our hard work of staying in careers, raising children, and doing all of the 'right' things couples do. Unfortunately, now I get to enjoy that by myself, without him, and that just plain sucks."

He explained that he didn't have those experiences. He had gotten married the first time at a young nineteen; both he and his wife were headed into the music business. Drugs and sex got in the way, particularly when his wife decided to have sex with other musicians in his band. That marriage had lasted less than two years. I could tell that it was very painful for him and that he was holding back the hurt.

Then he told me about how he found his spirituality through Hinduism a few years later and found a guru who provided him with balance. He remarried when he was thirty-four, having met his second wife at an ashram in New York. They had a son immediately after meeting, and both he and his wife loved following the practices of their guru. He then explained that somewhere along their journey, his wife became an alcoholic. He found himself raising his four-year-old son by himself, trying to create a semblance of stability. He had to put his wife into rehab several times, all of which failed. The three of them moved out here to the Bay Area to be with the ashram community after a stint in Michigan, where his wife's family resided. When things started to unravel in his marriage, he moved back to New York to live with his parents with his young son.

He smiled and grabbed my hand. I could tell that he was a very touchy person. He couldn't move around without touching me on the shoulder or grabbing my hand. We were sitting on the couch, and he started to kiss me oh so passionately. I loved the touch of his mouth on mine—that deep, penetrating soft kiss with the tip of his tongue gently exploring my mouth. Then his arms came around me with an all-encompassing, loving embrace. We adjusted to lying on my couch. I was so overwhelmed with this kiss that my mind said, *Just do it! This is good. You need this!*

I jumped off the couch and told him, "Just a minute!" I immediately went into the bathroom. I looked into my mirror to do a double-check, and my reflection told me, *You know this is your moment. Don't hesitate!* I washed my hands and then darted into my bedroom to make sure the condoms were close by. Then I went out into the hallway and waved him into my bedroom. "Come on," I said. "Come on into my bedroom." He moved quickly with the look and the bounce of a delighted little boy. His brown eyes were so gleeful, and he was smiling from ear to ear. We moved to my bed.

Afterward, I had an amazing feeling about me. He was a very passionate lover. He had kissed every inch of my body, gently and with the lightest kisses. He told me he loved women's bodies and cherished and loved worshiping them. I told him that it had been fourteen years since I had made love. He stopped his kissing and looked up at me. Then, his kisses seemed to intensify. My spirits just soared. *I'm attractive! How does this work?* I just enjoyed the moment, soaking in the experiences of love and passion. It had been so long, and I so enjoyed the feeling of love. When I rolled over away from him but was still in his embrace, I could feel the wetness of the tears coming from my eyes. I was overwhelmed with the sense of being whole again. I hadn't felt this type of touch or loving in such a long time. I don't know if he noticed those tears, but I sensed that he knew I was very emotional. He continued to hold me, softly breathing in my ear. I was in pure bliss.

He left a few hours afterward and promised he would call me in a few days, and he did. He would call me during the day when he was on the road at work. He was a courier for a law firm in Berkeley, taking papers to courthouses and setting up the courtrooms for the lawyers who worked in the room. He told me that he really enjoyed all the different courthouses and talking to the employees there. He would tell his jokes and bring smiles to their faces. Whenever he called me, it was always exciting, and his voice was full of energy. We had a lot of talks about spirituality. His dialogue was always a bit more passionate than mine, never hesitating in what he was asking for. He always asked questions directly. We had several weekends of passion—he stayed some weekends—and then Christmas was upon us.

I had told my kids in September that I would take their families to Disney World, so I rented a house in Orlando for the week after Christmas. I booked all of the flights and told both my daughter and my son (and his wife) that this was their Christmas and birthday gifts—all three were born in December. It was an event that had been planned for a long time; Larry and I had discussed it years before, saying that if we had the money, we would. It was a big expense, but I really wanted to make this trip memorable for my family. We were leaving the day after Christmas and planned to stay through the New Year, which was my daughter's birthday. After my son and daughter met Chris, they both called me asked, "Mom, he's not coming on our trip, is he?" I was surprised that they would ask me this and just replied, "Of course not! I just met the man, and what we have together is *not* what you think it is." I wanted this family trip to be special. Why include strangers?

So Chris and I had a wonderful, delicious day of Christmas in my apartment. I cooked up some magical food, and we just enjoyed ourselves. My family called between our love-making. My sister called to wish me a merry Christmas and could tell by the sound of my voice that I was enjoying myself immensely. She said, "You sound like a teenager to me!" I told her that I felt like one. I thanked her for my present; she had sent two nightgowns in one box. One was a comfortable and modest nightgown marked "Nice," and the other was a juicy negligee marked "Naughty." She got the message loud and clear.

> *Being deeply loved by someone gives you strength, while loving someone deeply gives you courage.* —*Lao Tzu*

CHAPTER 13

A Christmas to Remember

The day after Christmas, my kids, daughter-in-law, and granddaughters Haley and baby Betty flew out to Florida for our Disney World trip. That night we checked into our rented house, we stocked up on food and drinks and made some margaritas. I guess my kids had planned to question me, but I was just enjoying being in their presence and with my granddaughters. After a margarita, my daughter asked me, "So, Mom, tell me. Have you changed your will yet?" That question took me totally by surprise.

"What? Why would you be asking me this?" I was stunned at the question. I was not prepared for it since it had never entered my mind before.

"Well, we were thinking about this guy Chris and were wondering what plans you are making with him." I restated to them that we were simply friends who were dating and that any plans with him in my life are just premature.

Their conversation with me started to sour. I was there enjoying myself with my kids and grandchildren when a topic they wanted to vent about came up. I stopped myself short of becoming incensed and overreacting. *What is this leading to?* I thought.

As soon as I could, I went up to one of the upstairs bedrooms, put my meditation music on the iPod, and just tried to breathe. Why did I sense disharmony coming from my family? My inner being was pushing this into my mind, but I just breathed and let the thoughts go away. *Relax. We are all walking on eggshells. This will pass.*

On one of our designated days in Disney World, my daughter said something to my granddaughter, my daughter-in-law got upset about something, and I just wanted to walk away from it all—call a cab, go to a bar, anything. I just didn't want to be there with my family. Fortunately, I had rented two cars and told my daughter, "Take one of the cars and take Haley back to the house. Perhaps we are all tired and a little rest would help." She said she would, and I started to walk with my son, his wife, and the baby in the stroller. My daughter-in-law said something inaudible and looked totally upset, and my gut instinct was to just go back and catch up with my daughter. I told my son, "I think I'll join Donné and Haley. I'll see you later!" I didn't even look back.

That night, I called Chris and explained that I wished I weren't there and how close I was to hopping on an airplane and coming home. He told me, "If you had a guru, you could visualize his face and place your love there. Just remember to take in the breath." I knew that leaving wouldn't be good for the family dynamics, so I continued with the trip. I sensed that neither of my kids (nor my daughter-in-law, who was six months pregnant with baby number two) really enjoyed themselves. We ended up celebrating New Year's in the vacation home; no one was really in the mood to go out to celebrate. It was my daughter's birthday. Her boyfriend (or fiancé, at the time) was supposed to join us that week with his young daughter, but he never made it. So with her being upset about that, my pregnant daughter-in-law, and my son with all of the women in his life in a stew and moody, I understood full well why none of us enjoyed the trip. It was all bad timing. When I got home, I breathed a sigh of relief. I felt as if my obligation to my kids was over.

> *He who lives in harmony with himself lives in harmony with the universe.*
> —*Marcus Aurelius*

CHAPTER 14

A New Year, A New Beginning

After the New Year, when I got back to California, Chris came over for another fun weekend. He and I got to know each other better physically and mentally with each visit. He would comment on how well I had it, saying, "You and your husband really did everything right."

He talked about his family in New York and said that his dad's ninetieth birthday was coming up in February. His brothers were encouraging him to go, but he wasn't sure about it. He said that he felt pulled between being part of the family dynamics and the freedom of being away and enjoying his spirituality. He indicated some guilt that he had reneged on his responsibilities as a son and felt at fault about it. His younger brothers were there with his parents and would always be. So his obligation to his family was somewhat relieved because they were there.

He talked more about his guru and brought me books that he thought I might find interesting. My first thought when I

73

looked at one of the books was, *Is he trying to convert me to some cult-type religion?* We enjoyed each other's company in that cold January month. His birthday came up, and I gave him T-shirts with silly sayings. Some were a bit racy, but his humor matched the sayings.

He told me, "Why are you giving me this? I just don't give gifts and I am not good at it!"

I said, "Chris, I find giving gifts enjoyable. I'm not expecting anything in return; it's just the way I've always been." I thought, *what is* this *all about? Is he just frugal, or is he truly a person with no attachments to another? Or does he get worried about obligations?* I put those thoughts immediately away and cooked up some favorite light food. I was learning fast that he liked to eat simply. That Sunday night, he left me with a big, silly grin on my face as I watched him walk down the hallway from my apartment door. He said, "See ya," and didn't even look back over his shoulder.

When I reflected on that, I thought it was strange. It occurred to me that this man really wasn't romantic at all; he just enjoyed sex and talking about his guru. Really. What could possibly be attractive in that? I started reading through his recommended books and my own, pondering the self-inquiry of them all. I finished a couple of books that week while knocking time off at the gym, vigorously highlighting items I thought important to me (or to him?)

Halfway through the week, I got a call from Chris at midday. "Hi. This is Chris," he started. "I was driving all over the Bay Area today on my job, and suddenly I had to call you and ask you: would you come with me to my dad's ninetieth birthday in New York in mid-February?" That took me by surprise! He continued,

"I really like you and would love for you to meet my family. I know that they will love you." My heart jumped at the thought. I asked him about airfare and whether he had bought his ticket already. He said that he had just bought it a couple of days before and that it was a direct flight from Oakland to JFK Airport. I told him I would look up the fares and check it out, and then I'd call him back later. There was no offer to purchase my ticket. That was interesting.

When I hung up, my mind raced. *Wow. He likes me enough to meet his family? Is this leading to a relationship? But he didn't offer to buy the airfare, did he?*

I contacted the airline, which had reservations open, and found that the seat right next to Chris was available. I called him back and told him that I had gotten the flight reserved and was looking forward to meeting his family.

I decided to go visit my daughter and update her on my plans. I had been trying to figure out a source of additional income and thought that maybe selling a piece of property would help me find property back down in my new area. In some places, rent was actually more than what I could get in a mortgage. My daughter, being in real estate, might have a handle on it, I figured. I had talked to several of my new friends in the women's group, and they suggested different ideas.

When I got to her house, I took in my laundry that I had brought over. It was a nice way to spend the afternoon with her to catch up. She asked me about what I was doing, and the first thing I asked her for was advice about selling the land. "Mom, that is property that belonged to Grandpa. He built it; you can't sell it."

Wait a minute. Don't I own it? I thought I did; at least it was in my husband's and my name, so where was this coming from? My stomach knotted with a tight feeling, so I changed the subject to lighten the mood. I told her about Chris asking me to go to New York to meet his family. I was extremely happy right then. She then said, "You know, Mom, I have had him checked out. His credit rating is horrible. He has a record." I stopped her right there.

"What right do you have to check up on this man I'm dating?" I asked her. I was astounded. She replied, "Someone has to watch out for you. You are going through money like a teenager. In fact, you are acting just like a teenager that just had her cherry popped!"

I was flabbergasted. I started to back away from her and just told her, "Perhaps I'd better go. This discussion isn't where I want to be." Then I added, "Oh, and by the way, I did my own research on him and, yes, his credit isn't good because his son is backing out on a student loan that he cosigned for, and quite frankly, I think that this is *his* business and not something that *we* should be talking about."

She then started yelling at me. "Fine! Consider that you should not sell that property, and if you walk out of my house right now, I want the key to my house back." The drama accelerated from there, and I turned to get the key. I then stopped and told her, "If this is the way you want to part, that is fine, but I want the key back for my apartment, too, *now.*" We hastily exchanged keys and I drove away … dirty clothes and all.

Wow, I thought, *what part of that adult did I raise?* My husband and I had never fought like that and never in front of our children. Sure, we had some moments of disappointments with each other, but we were always civil with each other and neither of our children saw a lack of respect between us or with others. My daughter has always been a drama queen, but she was getting increasingly difficult to communicate with, especially since she "mastered" in the art of rapport and communication. Little did I know then, which I know now, that she had been dealing again with a seriously unstable person wallowing in his own story. They always take it out on the ones they love the most; I guess I was an easy mark.

It took me several days to figure out what had brought this out. But I couldn't console myself. I had no one to talk to. When I asked my new friends (all of them women with grown children) about this behavior, they all thought it was so odd. It gave me some justification that I had reacted just right. *Let it ride, Lori,* I told myself. *It will all work out soon.* But one thing I always quickly react to is when someone tells me that I can't do something. I was going to use that property as leverage to buy property back down where I was. *No more throwing money away on rent!* I concluded.

> *For every minute you are angry, you lose sixty seconds of happiness.*
> **—Ralph Waldo Emerson**

CHAPTER 15

Travel, Travel, Travel

Because our guy had won in the Presidential elections, all of the friends who went to the Democratic convention in August flew with me for a planned week in Washington D.C. for the Presidential inauguration and all the celebration. It was cold there, but OH, so much fun! We went to an inaugural ball, to museums, and just had a grand time. Near the end of the week, I was looking so forward to seeing Chris again. I put the misunderstandings of the argument with my daughter to the side.

I had a long talk with one of my friends, one who also had adult daughters. She told me, "Lori, each week, depending on the moods of my daughters, they either love me or they hate me. I finally came to the conclusion that I have no control of their feelings; I just have to make sure I feel good. So my only advice to you is, just be prepared."

She also said, "I finally had to agree with my husband that

loaning money to them when they asked for it or bailing them out of their situations just adds to the drama. We finally told them all, 'The Bank of Mom and Dad ' is now closed. Emotions cannot be part of the drama, and if you can't play by those rules, then don't come knocking on our door.'"

I sort of understood her. But then there I was, feeling a pull, and I told her, "Wanda, at least you have Craig there behind you. There isn't any way my daughter would have pulled this stunt if my husband was still alive." She said, "Hey, *my* daughters did it to us, and my hubby is still here. There is no way of changing the outcome."

I pondered her words for several days, making sure that what she experienced and what I experienced were not the same. But in reflection now, comparing my reality with her reality, I see that we, as the mothers, basically set ourselves up for these kinds of reactions by trying to overcompensate for one child and placating the other(s). It really was a no-win situation.

My birthday came up in early February, and Chris and I spent that weekend together. He even bought me a birthday card. When he handed it to me, he said, "I never do this, and it was so confusing to pick one out, so I bought two!" I thought that considering his simple way of living, this must have been a special event for him to be so thoughtful.

A few days later, we left for New York for me to meet his folks and his dad's ninetieth birthday party. He said, "My family is not into dressing up. This is just a birthday dinner at a restaurant honoring my dad. I know my family will love you."

His nephew, Mike, picked us up at JFK Airport. Mike looked amazingly Italian, with some similarities to Chris but in a different way. He took us directly to Chris's parents' house in the Bronx. It was an old house with three stories and wrapped in asphalt shingles. It had a small awning over the first step, which led into a small front yard surrounded by wire fencing. The street was narrow with cars parked in front of the homes and only a short block from the freeway.

When I walked into the house from the crisp, cold February air outside, a comfort and warmth swam over me. His mother, around the age of eighty-six, was small in frame but smiling from ear to ear, showing an inner brilliance of a woman who found life most amusing. I could tell that she stood her own ground with her family. His dad, though ninety years old, looked a bit gruff, but had an air of vitality that came through his personality. His eyes were piercing brown with the same glint that I could see in Chris's eyes. He smiled broadly when he met me. I could tell from their body language and enthusiasm that they were so happy to see their oldest son after about two years.

Chris immediately went into the kitchen and looked into the refrigerator like a little boy who made it home after school. He told me, "Lori, in this house, make yourself comfortable. No one will be waiting on anyone, so don't be shy if you need anything." His nephew asked about our luggage and where to put it, and Chris's dad said, "Carry it up to my room." I couldn't tell what the sleeping arrangements were going to be; Chris had never discussed it with me. There I was, a fifty-seven-year-old woman, wondering what his parents might think. Good grief!

We spent about five days there, and on several of them Chris went to a chiropractor nearby. He called this doctor a "network" chiropractor who practices a different modality for treatments. I had been going to chiropractors most of my life and had never heard of that type of treatment, but in the end, all chiropractors basically want to treat patients without the typical use of drugs. So we would take his dad's car to Larchmont, a small town just north of the Bronx, and he would get his adjustments while I walked around the duck pond out in front of the office.

Walking in that cold February air and seeing the ice over the water brought back memories of my life with Larry in Croton-on-Hudson. In our second year of marriage, we moved to New York to extend his education. It was a big adventure in our lives, both of us being born and raised in California and then moving clear across the country by ourselves. We only lived about thirty-five miles north of where I was standing at that duck pond.

The birthday party was held in an Italian restaurant in the Bronx, a favorite place for his dad. About twenty-five people were there, all family members or friends who counted as family. All of Chris's brothers were there, and I could tell from his reaction that he really did miss this part of his life. He later told me that it was tough for him to observe that his parents were getting older. I kind of thought, *At least you have your parents!*

It was a nice trip; his family was warm. Yes, we slept in his father's bed, which was difficult for both of us. I guess sleeping with someone else for a longer length of time than a Saturday night was awkward because it forced the acknowledgement that we were both set in our own ways with our own sleeping patterns. I wondered, *What would this be like if it were every night?*

I spent a full afternoon visiting with his parents as Chris went up and down the stairs of his old house, pushing and pulling something out of his parents' hallway closets. Out came an old drum set. He told his mom, "If Jamie comes to visit and he wants these, let him have them, but I'm taking a couple of them back with me to California." We talked about everything having to do with my family, and most of all, I took notes about their family. I had started a family tree for Chris, and his father was really glad when I showed it to him. He filled me in on the missing details, reminiscing about his family relations and looking at the tree. I could tell that he liked going over his history.

We packed the drums into bags, and as we were going out the door to head to the airport, his mother gave me a huge hug and his father said to me, "Anytime you want to be a part of this family, we will adopt you!" As we were driving to the airport, Chris said, "My dad said to me, 'You need to marry that woman!' And I told him, 'She wouldn't even consider it, Dad, because she would lose her widow's benefits." I just smiled to myself and thought, *Yes, Chris, that might be true, and I don't think I would ever want to marry again.* By the time we were headed out of town, I was *so* looking forward to my own bed!

When I dropped him off at his place, he gave me a big hug and a kiss and walked away with his tough guy walk, which I later realized, was because one leg was shorter than the other. As I watched him walk away, he turned and looked over his shoulder at me, and I got the feeling that this might be the end of our courtship, if one would call it that. I made it appear to his parents that he was a stand-up, solid guy, and their approval of me seemed to make them approve of him. I realized that thinking like that was a bit jaded and truly judgmental. Where was I going? Especially with this relationship? *Is it a relationship?*

And the time came when the risk to remain tight in a bud was more painful than the risk it took to blossom. —Anais Nin

---

CHAPTER 16

And Life Does Go On, or Does It?

After our trip to New York, Chris would call me intermittently and come out on weekends to visit. One of those weekends, he lamented that he was having some difficulty with his landlady and said that he was going to be looking for another place to live. We were getting along magnificently, and I offered him my second bedroom as an option. He looked at me with astonishment and said, "Are you sure?"

I said "Chris, I see our relationship has moved closer, and I really don't mind sharing my life with you. How do you see it?"

It took a few minutes of pondering; he thought about it and looked at the room. He came back and said, "You know, I am a really quiet person, when you get to know where I'm coming from." I told him we would share the rent, of course, and he replied, "Of course! I wouldn't think twice about it. Let me go home and consider it as an option. The ideal thing would be to find a place closer to my work." I said, "There is no pressure here. If you want to consider it, it is yours."

We continued to talk about where we were in our lives. His admired the fact that I had security. I could see that he was fun, and saw life freer than I ever had. He continued to question me, "don't you have any kind of spirituality? Don't you think that there is a God, or a guru that you can meditate or pray to?"

I explained, "Chris, I didn't have that for most of my adult life. I was married to a man who truly believed in the scientific side of life rather than religions. We didn't bring it into our lives, and this is truly a new area for me. I have read more self-inquiry books in my life just in these last two years than I did in over thirty years."

He looked at me, and said in what seemed like a judgmental way, "Well, it doesn't work for me if I can't have my guru, and that's what is most important to me." The dialogue started to sour.

I asked him, "Well, where is this relationship going? How is this going to reveal itself?"

He stopped and said to me very seriously, "There is no relationship here. We are just together as long as there is companionship and sex—nothing else. I think that maybe we need to consider the fact that we have differences in our spiritual beliefs."

With that said, I replied, "Then perhaps your moving in here is a bit premature. I'm sure you can find another place that will fit your needs. I know that your relationship with your landlady might be uncomfortable, but I'm sure that another place will work out for you that would fit you better." Those words came out of me very strongly. I hadn't used conviction with so much intensity before, as if I was removing someone from my life forever.

We agreed that was a better solution for him, and we mutually established that we would stay in touch. When I closed the door behind him, I looked out the peephole to watch him walk down the hallway. He was walking with more of an angry walk, with the Bronx-style hitch in his step. Not once did he look over his shoulder.

I sat down and decided then and there that it was important that I place myself as a priority. I was crestfallen. Somewhere in my brain, I had managed to drum up a "future" with this man. I had immediately sought out something or someone that I could distract myself with rather than working on myself. I was depressed, thinking that life just wasn't working out well. So I started writing on my doodle pad: *You are a worthy person, you are love, you have initiative, you are awesome, you are beautiful.* I would erase the words and then write again: *love, genius, compassion, worthy, happiness.* I continued to erase the words and then re-emphasize the feeling with more words. It did lift my spirits.

A couple of days later, Chris finally called me. His tone sounded like he wanted to talk, but there was some hesitancy in it. He finally said, "There is no relationship between us. The only relationship I have is with my guru and no one else." It sounded so final to me. We hung up, and it was more than a month before we talked again.

During that time, my sister-in-law, Diana, and I decided that we would attend a workshop being held in the San Francisco area. *The Art of Allowing* was a positive-thinking workshop held by Esther and Jerry Hicks, founders and authors of many books through their group called Abraham-Hicks. Their workshops brought groups of people together to ask questions regarding surpassing the negative aspects of life. It was truly the most uplifting workshop I had ever attended. Diana, like me, had been delving into the laws of attraction, and we both agreed that this would be something we might enjoy together.

Not only had she lost her brother, my husband, but she had also lost her mother five months prior to that. Both of us were seeking relief from grief, and what Abraham was saying on how we approach life as it unfolds truly resonated with us.

One of the most significant sayings that Esther Hicks said that sticks with me even today was this: *You didn't come to get it done. You didn't come to fix something that is broken. You didn't come to seek worthiness (you were never unworthy to begin with). You came for the thrill of the ride.*

It truly put in perspective my reality that I had always tried to fix whatever I saw as broken. This included any relationships with any and all persons who were a part of my life—my parents, my children, my husband, and my friends.

After buying several of the videos and reading several of the books, my life changed—significantly! I had come to the core of the laws of attraction: you attract what vibrational signals you put out.

I felt like a big sponge, just absorbing all the information I could about my defined purpose. I determined that from then on I would be a true student to this purpose and seek the life of joy that I so deserved.

> *The basis of your life is freedom; the purpose of your life is joy.* —*Abraham*

CHAPTER 17

Seeking Abundance and a Home

Because I was determined not to rent in the Bay Area for the rest of my life, I decided that I would look into the possibility of buying a place. I talked to one of my realtor friends about how I could do this. She had been in real estate for more than thirty years, and she knew of my dilemma and of my property up north. The post office that I had inherited and that was providing me with a little income had no liens on it, and she suggested that I make it work for me. So I took a small loan out on it and used the money as a down payment for a home in the Bay Area.

I found another realtor who worked with me several times a week, and one of my new Soroptimist friends was a mortgage broker. She managed to get me approved and ready to jump into the thriving real estate market for investors. It just seemed that the universe was delivering to me everything I focused on. Bay Area properties were sinking in the housing market because the unbelievable housing market bubble had finally burst. So I would look and look for a house, put in offers, and get rejected because package investors would buy the house out from under my offer. It was a heady time. I'd get my hopes up on one place and then get a call that it was taken.

I continued my dancing on Thursday through Saturday nights. I had had little contact with my daughter after her last outburst. I didn't want to get caught up in the drama of trying to explain my actions when she shared very little with me. She was losing her job in real estate market, and she managed to remove her husband from her life after several close, very nasty, drunken situations. I worried about what my granddaughter was witnessing, but I didn't want to get into another confrontation.

Chris started calling me again, and we saw each other occasionally. I still had a great fondness for him. It was one of those situations of needing companionship and, of course, the sex. He would call and tell me if he was coming through my area, and I'd invite him over for the night. It was becoming a typical "booty call" relationship. But we did share more about ourselves with each other, and I began to understand more about his issues with relationships. It seemed that the more I delved into self-inquiry, the closer I would get to that understanding.

He finally told me on one of those visits that he was sorry that he had used such drastic words with me. He apologized immensely, saying, "Lori, I am so sorry that my discussion with you about not having a relationship seemed so final. I think you now realize what I was meaning about 'relationship.' You really have to have one with yourself before you have it with another. It has been a slow process for me, and the closer I get to it, the more peaceful I feel." We would see each other about every other week. Sometimes I would call him if I was going to be over in the Oakland area.

He had moved closer to his ashram and was living in the community with which he was familiar. He had known many of the people who lived in the neighborhood for more than twenty years. Many from the New York ashram were now showing up in the Oakland ashram. He invited me to come to the ashram with him several times so he could introduce me to Siddha Yoga. I finally took him up on his offer and met him there. He walked me through the ashram grounds and building, showing me places where his son had played as a baby. He took me into the ashram, and we went into the great meditation hall. The guru's pictures were on the walls, with a large statue of an elephant in the back; he told me that the name of that god was Ganesh. He showed me the neighborhood homes that he, his wife, and his baby boy had lived in twenty years earlier. The homes were well kept, and rooms were rented out to most of the devotees of the ashram. It was a very communal neighborhood, and he seemed so at peace there.

I told him that I was in escrow for a home. I had told him several months before that I was going to actively pursue this goal, but to him it seemed like an impossible goal. I could see admiration in his eyes. He then told me that he was leaving his job to pursue his dream of being a full-time musician again. He said that he had injured himself at work and had been put on light duty, which he just hated. Somewhere in that discussion, I told him, "Chris, you know you can become of full-time musician. All you have to do is just allow it." The look on his face was one of amazement. It was as if he was seeing me as a different person. I proceeded to tell him that, according to the laws of attraction, you get back what you put out. That discussion was a significant turning point between us, both as lovers and as friends.

When I finally got the closing date, which would be in August, it was such a relief. I knew that I was no longer going to be "throwing money" into the rental market. Sure, the market was down, but I was truly getting a good deal. The monthly cost of buying the house was the same as the rent that I had been paying for almost two years in a small, two-bedroom apartment.

My son was still talking to me, but he was busy with his career and new baby. I didn't realize it at the time, but he too was about to lose his house. Both of my children were upside-down in their mortgages, and there I was taking advantage of someone else's loss and buying a house.

He and his wife invited Chris and me over to their house for dinner a couple of times. It was a warm and sweet environment. I was truly happy for my son and his new wife. I really didn't have much time to get to know her with all the turmoil in my life. They got married less than a year before Larry died and had the baby six weeks after he died. They both worked full time and didn't seem to be having difficulty paying for their home, but they were literally upside-down in the value of their home and had no other choice but to walk away from it. They had become victims of the housing crash.

It was ironic that I was buying a house while my two children were in the process of losing theirs. The world is not fair. But I was starting to see that with every downside, there were always other openings to opportunities. Perhaps this would be good for them too.

> *Doing what you love is the cornerstone of having abundance in your life.*
> *—Wayne Dyer*

CHAPTER 18

Dancing in Search of Joy

By the end of April, my son and his wife had their second daughter, born on Larry's birthday. Since their first baby had been born via caesarean, they opted to have this one the same way, choosing Larry's birthday for the delivery. Dan said that they chose that day to honor his dad, but my mind was saying, *Why can't the baby have her own day? Why does she have to share the day of someone that she'll never know?* They named her Clara, after her great-grandmother, Dan's grandmother. It's interesting that my mother-in-law actually hated her name. She had gone through life insisting to be called CJ rather than Clara.

The day of baby Clara's birth was stressful. First, my daughter was still barely speaking to me, and I knew she would be in the waiting room soon. Second, I was going through the motions of being the supporting mother and mother-in-law, but I was still having bouts of grief because Larry was not there to celebrate the birth of his third granddaughter. The good news is she was born healthy and beautiful, just like her sister, Betty. My daughter walked in and acted quite cold and distant toward me, but I figured that this would all pass. Or would it?

I was well on the way to finding myself. I found one self-help book after another and was consuming them like candy. I started actually dancing at Badabing's and having more fun than I had had in years. It had been eighteen months since Larry had left me. I began to be able to think about it more because of an intrinsic belief that he was still here with me in some way. As I got deeper into my understanding of what spirituality truly meant, I started to feel freer and lighter.

I would go to the dance club to listen and dance and watch the people playing their parts in their lives and with one another. Sure, there were cliques of people who knew each other well, but there was always someone new there, doing the same as me—finding his or her way in this weird social context of dancing and nightlife. Finding themselves in the midst of a social phenomenon called "night clubbing," most of them were seeking comfort in their drinking or a one-night stand.

I had never experienced it before. I went from college to marriage in a swift two-year period after I graduated high school. This was all new research for the newfound me! I observed the different characters on the dance floor and the ones standing back, just "observing."

So I would flirt, I was carefree, and I enjoyed myself and danced. And there were many men there doing the same things. I would look forward especially to Thursday nights because live bands performed at the club. Fridays and Saturdays were strictly DJ nights, but the same faces were there on those nights, dancing with carefree abandon. I felt safe, and I felt this was the joy I needed to experience.

One man was such a good dancer, and he swept me off my feet. He would hum in my ear and loved to salsa and rumba. His name was Jimmy; he was fifty-one years old, divorced, with a grown daughter and an eight-year-old son. He said he was a drywall hanger, currently not working because of an injury. I asked him if he meditated, and he told me that he had a few times in his life. He also said, "I come to Badabing's for the live music, the pretty ladies, and the fun in dancing," I flirted with him. He was about five-eleven and slender, with a very nice presence. He seemed to be a very mellow guy. As we continued our dancing, he would throw in another step, and I kept up with him! He would hum the words to the song lightly in my ear in the slow dances.

Jimmy was also black, and I loved to call him my "Nubian prince" (in my mind). I had never dwelled on the differences between the human races. Being raised a military brat, my upbringing had been pretty diverse. This guy seemed sweet, honest, and very present in the moment. The color of his skin didn't bother me; I just cared that he truly enjoyed the moment of dancing, flirting, and just having fun.

One night, I had him follow me home. It was an amazing experience. There I was with another man—someone who touched me, explored me, flattered me—and I felt no guilt or shame in what I was doing. I felt "naughty" to be doing the "nasty" with very little attachment. We had a couple of one-night stands, of which I came away from a feeling of detachment from him and I truly wasn't feeling any connection or future with him. And if size means anything, this man definitely supported the rumors. I remember being shocked when I first heard it as a young adult—the saying, "Once you go black, you never go back." But I suspect that my being a redhead fulfilled some fantasy of his too.

But then I started to think that there seemed to be something missing. He would follow me to my apartment when the music stopped at Badabing's. We would have some really nice sex, and then he would get up around four o'clock in the morning, put on his shoes, and just leave. Once, he told me that he had a job to go to, so I made sure he left on time. I had the odd sense of obligation to stay awake so he wouldn't oversleep.

During that time of sleeplessness, I would reflect on how my mother or my grandmother would react to me just then. With a man of another race? Not married, having a "booty call," and at the age of fifty-eight? (I bet they both were simply rooting me on.) I would watch the clock tick down in wakefulness, watching its numbers slowly move from 3:00 a.m. to 4:00 a.m. while he snored away. I finally accepted that there was no connection with him, just an opportunity for lust and adventure.

The dancing moved outside with the warm weather. Most of the people who normally showed up at Badabing's started going to the local Hilton. Many more people were there. The music was just as great, and the energy and vibration of fun filled the warm summer air. A few other men caught my eye. It was fun and a bit naughty, but I came to the realization that I really didn't have to answer to anyone. My parents were gone, my daughter was not speaking to me, and my son was holding silent vigil in his life, busy with his career and family.

In the mornings, after a workout in the gym, I would meditate for about sixty minutes, read, and then prepare for my dancing from Thursday through Saturday nights. Sometimes, when Chris would come around to visit, he mentioned that I had a different aura around me, one of sensuality and excitement. He also said that I seemed to "glow" and that he found that alluring; it attracted him to me more. It was strange to me that a man would enjoy a woman's dating other men and find her alluring and inviting because of it. He would get really excited when I would tell him about some of my "dates." It was probably life in general showing me that I can find joy and love in everything I do and that some people carried no judgment. One thing I did find out was that he had no judgments or inhibitions in the bedroom. He made no judgments of me—just smiling back at me was enough.

I decided that I probably wasn't the best as far as experience in the bedroom. So, when I came across a book in the spiritual section of the bookstore called *Tantric Awakening*, I thought, *Well, now, will this help me with my self-inquiry into my sexuality?* I bought it on the spot. I devoured it, reading about the journey the woman who wrote it was trying to obtain. She wanted to be a Tantric instructor. I tried to understand the meaning of the spiritual path of an individual and that of a couple.

The next time I was going to be with Chris, I prepared myself with light meditative music, incense, and a very intentional assertion that I wanted to try these methods with our lovemaking. He said, "I'm game if you're game!" And from then on, for a long time, I would use these methods and meditations when he came to visit. I felt that our sexual excitement was heightened. It seemed to have more meaning, and many times, when we were resting in each other's arms, I would close my eyes in meditation and see a blue light coming into my mind where my third eye was supposed to be. This new practice made some significant changes in me. One time, I told Chris about the blue light, and he just chuckled and said, "You know, Lori, you may become awakened before I do if this continues." He then smiled and kissed me tenderly.

Close to Father's Day, I sensed that Chris was missing something. He seemed to become more moody and melancholy when we would get together. Earlier, he had told me that he had not seen his son in a couple of years, so I decided to reach out and contact his son without Chris's knowledge. I introduced myself to him through Facebook and asked him to call me at a certain time. When he called, I told him that I was a good friend of his dad's and that maybe what his dad needed was a visit from him. I bought him a ticket from Boston to Oakland and told him that under no circumstances was he to tell his dad who flew him out. My outer self told me I was probably meddling in an area that I shouldn't, but my inner self told me this was the right thing to do.

I met his son at the airport, and we went out for lunch. He was taller than his father. His eyes were blue, not like his father's, but they still had that mischievous glint to them. He told me that lunch was his treat. He said that he was excited about seeing his dad and that he would forever maintain my anonymity. I took him to his dad's house without being seen, and just before he got out of the car, I said, "Remember, this is to be discreet. If I hear anything from your dad about how I was involved, I will deny everything. Make sure you enjoy this visit. It will be good for him too." He replied, "I don't know how I could possibly repay you for this." I simply said, "Remember to pay it forward. Sometime in your life, you will have an opportunity to try to make someone feel good. Just remember this moment and enjoy it."

I felt good about what I had done and kept quiet for three days. It was a short visit, but the Sunday night that I knew his son would fly home, I called Chris and asked him about his weekend.

He told me casually but with amusement in his voice, "Oh, my son flew out to see me for Father's Day. It was a nice surprise, but it just reminded me that he is like his mother." I asked, "Did you have a nice time with him?" He said, "Everything was fine the first night, and it was so wonderful to see my son. The second night he went out to spend with his friends in the East Bay Area, and he came back drunk. It was just a reminder that he probably has the same addiction that his mother has. It breaks my heart!" I could tell by his tone that he was more irritated than anything. My doubts about secretly providing that gift without his knowledge made me very unsure of my motives. What was I trying to prove by meddling in his family? I became discouraged and decided not to say anything more that might inflame his emotions.

When I hung up with him, I picked up my new book, *The Power of Now* by Eckhart Tolle, and started to delve into more self-inquiry. My mind was wandering while reading Tolle's profound words. *Why did I do that? What was I trying to prove? Did I bring on something worse than I intended?* I contemplated those questions, trying to figure out what was behind it all. It was a difficult path I had drawn for myself. How do I surpass this effort of helping someone else and not feel bad about the result? I had learned a lesson, realizing that, sometimes, you just can't control others' outcomes, especially if you seek their approval.

I reminded myself that my effort was intended to go unre-warded. The results of that effort were not my manifestation but someone else's that I tried to make happen. It didn't go well.

> *Live as if you were to die tomorrow. Learn as if you were to live forever.*
> —*Mahatma Gandhi*

CHAPTER 19

My Process of Creation

The rest of that summer was delightful. I was accomplishing something that I had set out to do—buy a house. The market was really perfect, what with the unfortunate economic situation. I didn't have much money left, but it was enough to get into the market back in the Bay Area, where I had been much of my adult life. I was driving up Highway 101 to southern Humboldt periodically, getting my nature fix, getting melancholy with my memories with my husband there. Being in escrow—it was a short sale and the paperwork was in the hands of the banks, which might take forever to complete it—my anxiety about doing this on my own developed into a panic. Was this buyer's remorse?

I instinctively knew that this was the best thing for me to do: keep the house up north to visit occasionally and live in the house in the Bay Area permanently. I had slight hesitation about the house that my offer had finally been accepted by the banks. This doubt was based that I was moving back into the neighborhood where I had history in raising my family and living my life with Larry, but I knew it was the right thing to do, so it was a long, patient wait for all the t's to be crossed and the i's dotted to finally make it happen.

After driving the five hours up 101 and then back to the East Bay Area, I always had an odd sort of "Where am I?" feeling when I would wake up. *Am I in Dublin? Am I at the ranch house?* I would think upon waking in the morning. It was almost nauseating at times, throwing me off until I could fully wake up.

It always seemed that after being at the ranch house, driving home to the Bay Area was so automatic for me. I'd throw my cats in the car (with a litter box in the back) and hit the road with nothing but the bare minimum in the car because I had fully stocked homes at each end. The hardest part was rounding up the cats to get them back in the car. I usually would stay at the ranch about a week to ten days, and they would get comfortable there. But the minute they saw me packing up my small suitcase, I couldn't find them! One time, I got one of my cats, Sneakers, in the car, and the other one, knowing the area better, found a place to hide. In the house, I could drive him out of each room, closing the doors behind me and finally cornering him in a hallway. This time, the game was outside—bad thinking on my part. It took me forty-five minutes to catch him and load him in the car. He did not want to go on this five-hour drive!

I started to get pretty organized after that episode and would pack the car the night before I planned to leave. I would quietly move my items into boxes and prepare them for loading first thing in the morning. I would lock the cats in the garage that night and then, first thing in the morning, just hop in the car after cornering them in the garage and lifting them into my car. The cat carrier would work fine until Sneakers would throw up or have an accident. Of course, Smokey, the other cat who never did get sick would want out. I would have to let them both out into the car to wander as I drove down the highway. Once they settled onto the passenger seat, they would be happy.

My trip down to the Bay Area was full of music or audios from Esther and Jerry Hicks. I noticed that when I had my dance music on, the cats (or Sneakers at least, the most sensitive one) would just meow and meow. But when I put on the audios of Esther and Jerry Hicks with Esther talking from her "Abraham perspective," the cats would always just settle down for the rest of the trip as long as those audios were playing. I got a lot of advice and insight from the dialogue on the audios. It resonated with me stronger and stronger as I saw that I truly was creating my own reality, as we all are. If I choose to create drama, drama will come to me.

I always felt the pull to visit Chris before driving on home to Dublin. He lived on the edge of Berkeley in Oakland, and I could hop off the freeway and visit briefly. His roommates had left for the summer, so he had the house to himself. It became a booty call for me to stop by, talk, make a little love, and just go home happy. He truly enjoyed it too, because afterward, we would talk about the content of my audios and he would share his Siddha Yoga readings and teachings with me.

He was out of work by then and collecting state disability for his injuries. He was so unsure of where he was going in his life. He was fifty-nine, soon to be sixty in January, and was going through a bit of anxiety of his own. We became familiar with our insights on each other, and it was comforting to share this with someone else. The issue of a "relationship" never became a topic for us. It was an "open" relationship that was more comfortable for him and that I was getting used to. After all, I was still seeing Jimmy occasionally at Badabing's.

On August 1st, I moved into my house. Moving day for me marked a big chapter in my life. My brother and his wife came over the day I moved in; boxes were all around me. I opened a bottle of champagne to celebrate my new place, and my sister-in-law looked at me with such a look of awe and said, "I just realized that this is probably the first time in your life that you have made such a life-changing decision by yourself, isn't it?" I took a deep breath, deeper than most, looked at her, and said, "Thank you for noticing. You are absolutely right. I had not thought of that until you brought it up just now. I was just plodding along, doing things that I thought I needed to do. It seemed almost like I needed to do this." They both looked at me and raised their glasses. My brother lifted his glass and said, "Congratulations, Lori. You have just entered a new chapter in your life!" We clinked glasses and said, "Here, here!"

I spent several weeks "nesting"—painting, moving, unpacking, making my house to my liking. My daughter called and wanted to know if I wanted some Haley time. I was ecstatic; I said, "I would love to see her. Please bring her by!" I guess this was her way of checking out my new neighborhood. My granddaughter's father lived in my new town, so it was convenient to see her when he would have one of his weekends with her. My daughter showed up, and Haley stayed overnight with me in my new home. I could tell she was uncomfortable. She felt the stress between her mother and me. Children seem to have an instinctive sense about these things. It was a brief visit, but I knew that somehow she could understand that her Nana was okay and things were safe and secure.

I went out front of my new house, trying to figure out how to get things tidied up. The watering system had been turned off months before, and most of the landscaping was close to dead. I pulled weeds and finally got a phone number for a gardener from my good friend who lived in the same town. He was there almost immediately. For a steep price, he cleaned it all up in about five hours, put in new bark in the front areas, and checked all the sprinkler systems. Ah, it was all starting to come together. I hired him on the spot to come in on a regular basis.

That afternoon, I put myself in the shower, fussed myself up, and drove the thirty-seven miles to the Hilton that night to continue my dancing. Moving so far away from my dancing places was not an advantage, but it truly felt so good! I celebrated with some shots of Patron. I danced and danced and was having a wonderful time celebrating my new life. Several men came up and asked me to dance. One who had introduced himself as Frank. He wasn't very tall, slight built and had a long braid coming down his back. He put out a fun energy that attracted me to him.

We went outside to talk. I told him about my process of seeking happiness, and then he shared his story. He loved motorcycles. He had been a professional motorcycle racer and had about a hundred of them stored in a storage container. As we talked, he shared with me that he needed to sell them because he had been swept up in a physical problem and had not been able to work. He then showed me his arms and was scratching them. They were raw with flaky, dry skin. I continued to talk to him about stress and asked what he had done to get health care. As is the case for most people without jobs, he didn't get any health care.

As the night continued, we flirted a little and he even rubbed my feet because of all the dancing we were doing. *Oh,* I thought, *a man who likes to rub feet?*

My fun night with him was not one of physical attraction but of giving him advice about his situation and feeling sorry for him. He told me that he was sleeping on his daughter's couch. He had no home, an old RV that was stored, and a complex story about the hundred motorcycles. He asked for my phone number, and I told him, "Frank, I normally don't give out my phone number, and I'm not ready to do that ... but perhaps you'll be here next week?" He said, "I'm looking forward to it!" So he walked me to my car and watched me drive away. I got home, fell into my bed, and just felt more euphoria about what was coming my way.

The next morning, I went out to the front of my house to look at what else needed to be done. The neighbor across the street was mowing his front lawn and waved at me. He stopped his mower and walked across the street. I noticed that he was tan and had wavy hair braided down his back. He build was quite impressive; muscles showed on his arms. He reached to shake my hands and introduced himself. "Hi, I'm Nigel LaFollett. I'm your neighbor here and want to welcome you to our neighborhood." I asked him how long he had lived there, and he replied, "Since the houses were built, about sixteen years." He was so friendly. He took off his sunglasses, and I noticed his very green eyes. He had such a big smile.

I smiled back at him, and he said, "You've met Don and Terri, our other neighbors, right?" I told him, "Yes, Terri came over and introduced herself to me a couple of days ago. It's really nice to have such warm and friendly neighbors." He said that he was happy that the house I bought was not a rental and that he was glad that someone was living in it. He then explained that he knew the previous owner, who had lost the house. She had been friendly and would always cook him dinner for helping her around the house. "She was a single lady who didn't have a lot of talent doing things to her house, so I was always happy to help her for a meal or two!"

I then asked him, "So you don't cook?" He explained in his New Orleans accent, "No. I'm single too, and cooking is not something I relish, so I will do handy work for a lot of friends so I can get a cooked meal or two." Then he said, "So you and your husband both work?" I proceeded to tell him my story of widowhood, that I was semiretired, and that, no, I didn't have a husband. Then I asked, "Why did you think I had a husband?"

"Well, I saw you outside a month ago before you moved in, and you were talking to a man in front of your mailbox. I just figured that was your husband." I thought about that and then realized that I had been standing outside with the realtor when we were going over the things in the house that needed to be corrected, including the leaning mailbox. I said, "No, I'm here by myself on my new journey of home ownership. It's great to know that a handyman is nearby. I might offer you the same deal—food for some help with a few things that I can't do."

He was so enthusiastic. He said, "Well, I just would be so happy to help a lady in need! I love the do-it-yourself projects. I look forward to those." Then I asked him about a few things in the house that I couldn't figure out. He said, "Well, if you don't mind, show them to me. Perhaps I can shed some light on the subject."

He followed me into the house, and I proceeded to ask him about several things, including the stain in the guest bathroom. He told me about a pipe problem with the toilet that the previous owner couldn't resolve and said that he had come to her aid when water was running down the hallway.

My heart was beating so fast with this good-looking guy standing there—single, green eyes, polite manners, willing to do handyman jobs. My husband had been such a handyman. There were few do-it-yourself people out there, and here I found one again! *Thank you Universe!*

I asked him what he did for a living, and he informed me that he was retired from the post office. He said that he was fifty-seven and had taken an early retirement to enjoy the benefits of his thirty-seven years with the U.S. Post Office. "How neat!" I said. "You and I are both retired!" He smiled broadly and said, "You know, I think your moving into this neighborhood has just spiced up our street. Welcome home!"

I showed him out the door and promised him that I would very likely use his services when my projects came up. As I closed the door and watched him cross the street, I thought, *Wow! When you ask for something, somehow it truly is delivered! Here was a very nice man who has manners AND is nice looking!* I locked the door and went back to meditate on this.

A hard man is good to find.
—Mae West

CHAPTER 20

Moving through the Steps of Living

I settled into my new neighborhood with a ton of appreciation that I had followed a path of trying to "right myself." I had the outside of the house painted and the inside half-painted—trying to save the money for other things that I knew had to be done. I rolled up my sleeves and painted walls, power washed the fence, polished the windows, and watched the leaves start to fall.

One day, I decided to pull out my ladder to clean the gutters. I was standing on the very top, mask on my face and goggles on my eyes, pulling out the old leaves and debris that had been there several for years. I was a sight! I heard a voice below me; it was Nigel, standing there and staring straight up at me. I was so intent on getting the leaves out of the gutters that I had not heard him come across the street.

He was smiling up at me and said, "Good morning! I couldn't help but see you on that ladder. You are dangerously close to falling, and I would hate to be witness to that, so I thought I'd come across and catch you, just in case you did fall!"

I stopped and looked down at him with doubt and surprise. Geez, I must look horrible! I thought. I'm sweaty, my hair's a mess, goggles, mask—what must I look like? Is this my Sir Gallahad? A knight in shining amour? I stopped what I was doing and got down off the ladder, apologizing for my look and attire.

"You know, I have to admire a woman who wants to do things by herself! I love projects like this, and you must let me help you with these things. That way I can get a free dinner!" I smiled at him and started putting away the bucket of leaves and folding the ladder. "Here, let me do that for you. Where do you want to place the ladder?"

I showed him where to put the ladder in my sparse garage and then told him, "Nigel, let me look around for projects, and I will treat you to a home-cooked dinner. How about tonight? You come over, have dinner, and we can go over some items."

"What time?" he replied. "I will definitely be there with all my smiles!" We set a time for 6:30 p.m. I smiled to myself as I watched him walk back to his house across the street. It was nice to hear such compliments from someone who wasn't from the Internet, on e-mail, or out on a dance floor. Those compliments seemed so artificial compared to this guy.

With the distraction of his visit, I realized that I had not finished the cleaning of the gutters, so I took out the ladder and finished the job. After that project, I went in to check out my refrigerator for what could possibly be a dinner. I selected chicken, rice, and asparagus for my guest and put a bottle of wine in the refrigerator to chill. Then off into the shower I went.

When Nigel arrived around 6:35 (okay, so I'm a bit silly about timeliness, but my mind said, Is this a quality or tendency, or has he planned to be slightly late?), he rang the doorbell. Greeting him at the door, I noticed that he had spruced himself up and was fresh from the shower, looking tan, fit, and appealing. I let him in and directed him toward my kitchen. He hadn't been in my house since his first visit and made a few comments on how great the house looked. He shared with me some of the fix-it jobs that he had helped the previous owner with. I took him directly toward my backyard and we went over the sprinkler system, which was old and broken in places.

"You know, I can really help you with this system." I noticed that he emphasized help with a lot of enthusiasm. I smiled at him and said, "This is all new for me. I was so fortunate to have a man in my life who loved projects like this. I'm finding my way around the art of assembling, fixing, and procrastination! It's nice to know that I have a neighbor who can show me the ropes on these things."

He then said, "I don't cook at all, and many of my assistances will require you to provide me with some food. I bet you know how to cook really well!"

"No problem, Nigel," I replied. "I am so ready to barter with you on that!" I then showed him some of the other things in the backyard that needed to be looked at. I asked him if he would like something to drink, like some wine. He said that he didn't drink wine or hard liquor but that his favorite beverage was Miller Lite. I mentally changed my shopping list.

We went back into my house, and I served him dinner. He was so grateful for it and thoroughly enjoyed the food. We talked about my widowhood and my children and granddaughters. He made me feel comfortable; he was attentive when I was talking. His demeanor was soothing and charming. He talked with a bit of a Southern accent. He had been born in Louisiana and had that Southern sweetness. After we ate, we talked about a time that he could come back over and show me how the drip irrigation system worked in my yards and a couple of things that he could help me with.

I also wanted to know if he liked to dance, if he had been married—simple things. He said, "I love listening to soulful music, but no, I'm not much of a dancer." He told me that he had never been married but had lived with someone for almost fourteen years. He told me that she wanted children but that he had never really wanted them. He also told me that he was enjoying his freedom and loved being a bachelor. Other than the inability to cook for himself, he felt he was doing quite well. We discovered that we were born in the same year, so we had a lot more in common given our generational point of view.

When I closed the door behind him, I wondered why the universe would send such a nice neighbor to me. I knew that somewhere, there was a plan. What it was, I wasn't quite sure, but I was definitely going to participate! So after he left, I decided to have some great dancing fun the next day and was looking forward to it.

> *Somewhere, something incredible is waiting to be known.* —Dr. Carl Sagan

CHAPTER 21

Nesting and Growing

My mind was on the process of making my new home seem a little fuller and moving certain things down that would feel more comfortable. I had one big empty bedroom and was seriously thinking that perhaps I could rent out that room, have company and gain some income. My mind was becoming very creative!

After moving in and all the painting and nesting, I had moved in and unpacked my meager boxes from the small apartment. I stood and looked at my new home, empty and in need of filling. I decided that I would drive up to the ranch house on Sunday and proceed to bring some of the items down for my house. I prepared myself for dancing that night and hopped into the shower.

Today was Thursday, and I really, really wanted to dance. When I got to the Hilton that night, the music, the people, and the energy just put me in a blissful state. I was enjoying myself. Frank, the motorcycle guy walked up and said to me "I'm so glad you are back!" He proceeded to buy me a shot of patron....my favorite dancing medicine!

So we danced, and flirted, and I was feeling so awesome. Somehow, the next thing I realized, he and I were headed back to my house. He was saying how he missed sleeping in a bed. He was still sleeping on his daughter's couch. Me....well, I was in just the right spirit, told him "Why don't you come home with me? I have enough room, and then tomorrow I'll drive you back to your truck". I smiled naughtily at him. He naughtily smiled back.

So an evening of fun turned into an all-nighter at my house. We were enjoying the moment and I thought, *Wow, what kind of woman have I turned into now? What would my friends think? Where is this life going?* I decided to "bless" the thoughts and just play out the hand that I had dealt myself. After all, I was a single woman with the smarts and the resources in front of me to make a happy life.

When I woke up the next morning, there Frank was all snuggled in my bed. He really looked so happy, actually smiling in his sleep. A pang of guilt hit me. What was I attempting to do? I knew that this guy wasn't going to be the right match for me—if there even was such a match. I thought, *If I were a guy, I wouldn't think twice about this hookup.* I looked at the clock; it was 11:00 a.m., and I didn't want this to become an all-day thing, so I made some breakfast and went in to wake him.

I went back into my bedroom, and he was sleeping so hard that I couldn't wake him up. I looked at his face, which seemed pale, and I wasn't sure that he was breathing. I shook him hard and said, "Frank, it's getting late. You need to get up so I can drive you back to your truck."

He finally opened his eyes and looked at me with amazement

in his blue eyes. "Lori, this is the most comfortable bed I have ever slept in, I'm finding it hard to get out!" He managed to get his feet on the floor. I fed him breakfast, and he was so thankful for the opportunity to sleep over.

On the drive back to his truck, we talked again about his selling his motorcycles, creating a website, and maybe auctioning them off. I could only suggest things that he could do, but I didn't step in to help him. I assured him that he was going to be fine once he had made decisions about his health and living arrangements. I definitely did not want him to even think he could come back to my place. After all, it was just a sleepover, and that was it.

As I pulled up to the side of his truck, I felt awkward, because I knew that I didn't want to see a replay of this. He asked me if I was coming back the following Thursday for dancing, and I said, "I have no plans for next week because I need to take another trip up to my house up north, so let's just keep in touch." He then asked for my phone number, and I gave it to him. He said he might want to ask me some more questions about selling his motorcycles. We gave each other a kiss, and he got out of my car.

How do I approach this? What did I learn from this? I knew I was exhibiting independent behavior. Was this the true me? A sex-starved tramp who went nilly willy around the dance floor? I felt myself shift at that moment. I said to myself, *Who in the world am I hurting? No one! I am enjoying this freedom and will do whatever I want at this moment and at this time!*

That afternoon, I continued painting my rooms. I put on my music loud and just enjoyed the process of "doing" things to this house that was all mine. I didn't have to ask anyone else's opinion or make a compromised decision about the colors of each room, where to put the furniture, and how to arrange it. I never had those problems with Larry, but I always had to consider the other person in my life. I reflected on my ability to find another home for myself and move on in my new life of expansion. I cranked the music to a very high volume and was dancing all over my home.

That evening, I prepared to go up to my other house to bring some items down. I carefully packed my car without my cats' knowing what I was doing. I was onto their trick of getting "lost" in my house before the trip. Trying to round them up and put them into my car was always a task. When people talk about "herding cats," I laugh at my ability to outsmart my feline friends.

The drive up was beautiful. I had my music going, and my Bluetooth receiver started ringing. I turned off the music and pressed the button.

"Hello?" The phone number wasn't familiar to me.

"Hello. Is this Lori?"

"Uh, yes," I answered. "Who is this?"

"Hi, Lori. This is Frank! I know you're on the road up to your other house, but I just wanted to touch base with you and thank you so much for that lovely night. I really enjoyed your company and just wanted to let you know what a warm and beautiful woman you are."

"Thank you, Frank," I said. "We do have fun, don't we?" I was trying to make the one-nighter stay that way, and I was already having misgivings about giving him my phone number.

"I also wanted to ask you a question," he continued. "Every year, around the middle of November, there is a large group of motorcycle clubs that go on this weekend trip down Highway 1 to Los Angeles, where they all meet. I would love to have you go with me. I'm sure you'll enjoy the beauty of Big Sur and the fun of the people around us."

Okay, now I'm going crazy. The visual of me in motorcycle leathers, being someone's bitch on the back of his Harley, made me laugh hysterically at myself inside. Listening to him talk, I was driving down the road thinking, *Here I am, a grandmother, albeit a young-thinking fifty-eight-year old, but I don't even have leathers! He's asking me to ride on the back of a Harley.* Just thinking about riding a motorcycle for two or three days with my legs spread over the back of a bike had me grimacing. "Frank, I'm flattered you would even think of me," I said. "Good grief! I don't even have leathers to ride in! I'm sure you have another friend somewhere who would love to go with you."

He talked to me a little more, and then I needed to close the discussion quickly. "Frank, I'm about to lose my cell service, so I'm going tell you again—I'm so flattered that you asked me, but I'm going to pass on this privilege. If I have a moment to talk to you later, I'll give you a call up at my other house. Cell service doesn't work well up there, so if I call it will be from the phone up there. So thank you and good-bye. If you don't hear from me, I'll see you at the Hilton soon enough."

When I pushed the button to disconnect the call, I felt a bit of a relief. I thought, *Well, there you go. You ask and it's given.* However, Frank was not exactly what I was asking for. He was fun to be with, but my inner self was just telling me that I needed to cool it on this one. I put on my music and continued up Highway 101 toward God's country.

When I arrived at the ranch house, it seemed so still, quiet, and cold. A small group of cows was huddled down in the "potato field," a spot just below our house where the Anzini family would plant potatoes before and during the Depression. I turned on the pilot light for the gas stove, wiped down the cobwebs outside the house, and filled up my bird feeders, including the hummingbird feeder hanging outside the kitchen window.

I cleared out the old phone messages on the answering machine. A few of my customers from my computer consulting business were asking if I could tend to their computer problems, so I decided to tend to their needs, make some pocket change, and stay for ten days. When I called them back, they were so happy that I was there. I scheduled some days to visit their homes. It was fall, the perfect time for reflection. My cats were happy, and Smokey (also known as "the hunter") immediately brought to my door a mouse, evidence that the field critters knew that they had been gone. As I watched him devour it, I told him what a good kitty he was. I knew that buying the house down in the Bay Area was the right move. Being up here made me melancholy.

I walked out into my front yard. We had lovingly put it together and planted roses, lavender and rosemary throughout the yard. The old Toyota was parked in the driveway. It had been Larry's truck. It didn't have four-wheel drive, and had only been used for hauling trash to the dump. This was his truck, the one he bought one day with extra money we had from a tax return. He loved it. I looked at the old Toyota pickup in the driveway and realized that I needed to make a decision on it. Taking it down to the Bay Area and selling it would be a good idea, it would help move me forward. I patted it and touched it, knowing that was the right decision. Sometimes I felt good by removing old memories. When I got back in the house I called and invited my sister-in-law Diana to come and visit me.

The house was warmed up, I had tea on the stove, and it was wonderful to visit with her. We caught up on things going on in our lives and reflected on what we were doing to make our lives more positive. We really enjoyed sharing the process of what we had been learning about the laws of attraction, in particular with Esther and Jerry Hicks. I asked her about the holidays and what was going on, specifically if she had any travel plans. We decided then and there that we wanted to go on a cruise together. It was an impulsive move, but we were so excited when we found a cruise to Mexico that would have four days of Abraham-Hicks workshops on it. Without any hesitation, knowing this was something we both needed, we booked it online right then.

The next morning, I drove down to one of my customer's business, the local general store, and helped her with a small network issue. I also checked in with the postmaster at the post office to make sure that any maintenance issues had been taken care of. Larry and I had received the post office as part of his mom's estate.

Then I went into the garage of our ranch house, which was definitely his domain. Larry was such a master in fix-it. He had a tool for everything, and a lot of things in that garage were foreign to me. Right before he passed away, my son and daughter and her then husband came through the house to help me pick out items I would need for my "temporary" apartment.

There was a weed whacker, a hedge trimmer, drills, drill bits, plastic PVC for the drip irrigation, and electrical parts—all tools that were still needed for that remote house in the boonies. Through determination and my many trips up to the ranch house, I was gradually making my way through the boxes and drawers with successful detachment.

I opened one of the cabinets and found a filing box. I didn't recognize that box, so with curiosity, I opened it and looked at the file folders. I quickly realized that Larry had done what I had been nagging him to do for years. The way each folder was marked in his small, scratchy handwriting, I knew that this had been done probably a few months before he died. There were thirty or forty folders, each meticulously marked with a label. One was marked "Water filters." Inside the folder was the label of the water filters used for filtering our tank water. Another folder was marked "Drip irrigation," and inside it was the warranty for the drip irrigation control box, the brand, and a map of each section of the garden that we had drawn out several years before. It showed one meter marked "front of house" and included the hand-drawn markings of each meter, where the pipe was laid, and how much it cost to set it up. Another folder marked "Washer, dryer" had warranty information and the maintenance brochure for each appliance we had purchased and used in the house.

I sat down on the stairs in the garage in wonderment at this box. I had nagged and nagged Larry for several years about what would happen if he was no longer here. How would I even figure out how things were put together? This was one of those "surprises" that I have heard about widows finding. It wasn't a stash of money in a sock somewhere or long-lost stocks tucked away, but the value of that box was just as priceless to me.

Figuring all of that out was so overwhelming that I shut the door to the garage, went into the house, and opened up a bottle of wine after turning on the music and just enjoying the view.

I contemplated all of the "stuff" that I had to go through by myself. It seemed that there was a sense of release going on inside me that I couldn't put my finger on, but scheduling the cruise with my sister-in-law actually made me feel better. As I sat on my deck, drinking the wine and savoring the taste and the view, I also started to contemplate my future. I still was meditating daily and, after each session, I found a renewed energy in myself. I also thought of the dancing that I had been doing, how good I felt, and my visits with Chris. I so enjoyed being with him; he was so silly sometimes, and he made me laugh most of the time. Whenever we went out to enjoy live music, it seemed we attracted others who were in a higher level. Happiness and joy seemed to gravitate toward us.

I also thought about his discussions with me about his spirituality and my slow but progressive feeling that spirituality probably was something I needed to at least experience. I got on the Internet and looked up his ashram website. They were having an "intensive" for a full Saturday. It was an all-day event, including being introduced to the lineage of gurus, chanting, and celebrations, so I thought, *Why not?* I decided that I wouldn't tell Chris that I was attending and surprise him, or at the very least let him know about it at the very last moment.

He worked in the kitchen daily doing "seva" in the ashram community. The roommates in his house were all devotees like him. They had a community of supporters of their guru, and it truly seemed like maybe it was time for me to put my toes in the water. So I booked my day of intensive there for the first weekend in November.

Smiling to myself, I felt like something good was happening again. It had been a great trip up to the ranch house. It seemed that two years after Larry's passing, things were starting to come together for me. I felt a great sense of gratitude. I went out onto my deck in the night again, raised my glass of wine to the sky and the tree line, and said, "Thank you, Universe! You are truly showing me a way, and I am ever so grateful!" I don't know if it was my imagination, but the tree line sort of lit up with an aura of energy around it. I knew that the universe was acknowledging that it heard me.

> *When you arise in the morning, think of what a precious privilege it is to be alive, to breathe, to think, to enjoy, to love.*
> *—Marcus Aurelius*

CHAPTER 22

Press Here to Continue

By the time I packed my car up with things to take down to the Bay Area home and got my cats back in the car, it was late in the day. It looked like I would be getting there later than I had anticipated. My big cat, Smokey, somehow escaped out the car door while I was trying to shove the other cat into my car. I had sort of planned out a way of getting them into the car, and it failed. Smokey would run under each porch and deck while I was chasing him around the outside of my house. I had already chased him through the house, closing the doors to the bedroom to try to corral them into a hallway. I finally opened up another car door, and he hid under the bumper of the car. Finally I grabbed all eighteen pounds of his cat body and threw him into the car. *Mental note: figure out how to fool these cats into believing that I'm not getting ready for the five-hour drive.*

I stopped at the top of the drive and walked in to say good-bye to Diana. I promised her that I'd come back up to visit and check out the house again before Christmas. Now that the weather would be getting colder, I printed out a checklist for the kids to use whenever they came up to the house: "1. Turn pilot light off on the gas stove. 2. Take garbage with you. 3. Turn off the thermostat." Then I followed my own steps after a quick vacuum of the house. I loved thinking of how clean it would be when I would open the door on my next visit up. It made the trip worthwhile.

As I was driving down Highway 101 towards the Bay Area, I put on my music and drove as if I was on automatic pilot. Every curve in the road had familiarity. I had a great sense of euphoria with me. Diana had given me a couple more audios of Abraham Hicks and that would give me about three hours of listening as I drove the 250 mile drive. The cats were peaceful in the back of my SUV, listening. When the CD's ran out, I put on my dancing music. I was feeling so exhilarated! (And of course, when the music came on the cats started meowing loudly, letting me know their option of my selection of music.)

I drove to my home, unloaded more "stuff" and my very happy cats that were so happy to be home, rolled up my sleeves, and started painting my rooms again. It was a Wednesday night; tomorrow was Thursday, and dancing sounded so good to me!

The next morning was the beginning of a beautiful day. I decided to unpack the items I had brought down from the ranch house. I had a bookcase, an end table, and a few more floor lamps. My phone rang; it was Chris, and he wanted to see how I was. He had a gig and wanted to know if I'd join him on Halloween night. This was the first time he had asked me to come and watch him perform. He knew the band members very well and had performed with them before. He managed to be a sit-in drummer, available for local bands to call on him for a performance when their regular drummers couldn't make it.

I asked him, "Will I need to wear a costume?" He said, "I hope so, and it will probably be sexy!" I purred to him on the phone like a cat and reminded him that he could come out and visit me anytime he wanted. He laughed and said, "Ooooh, you know I like pussies!" *I think I'll just call him "Nick Nasty" for now!* I thought. I laughed out loud at him and told him that I would be looking forward to seeing him then.

I wanted to tell him that I had confirmed my attendance of the intensive at the Siddha Yoga ashram that he attended, but I kept the words out of my mouth. I knew that my telling him what I was doing was going to release my power of taking the intensive and finding out for myself if this was an area of spirituality that I might want to experience. It was like I was putting feelers out to touch a religious element that I had put off for so many decades. I knew instinctively that telling him that I was attending would color his judgment of my intentions. It might send him the message that I might be meddling to get close to him. I knew that wasn't true, but I realized that this man was passionate about his practice and that he so wanted to share it with others. So, I quietly kept it to myself, knowing that in a couple of weeks I might let him know I'd be there just in case I ran into him there.

I decided to do some outside work around my house, checking on the landscaping that was finally catching up with water. The water to the house had been turned off for almost a year. Once I moved in and got the outside sprinkler system working, the landscaping around the house was finally starting to make a comeback. I decided that I needed to yank out some of the dead plants and put in some new ones.

After my trip to the gardening store, I put on my old clothes and started digging in the flower beds. I had put on my headphones to my iPod and was dancing around to the beat and working with the soil. Loving every moment, I was pulling the weeds out and digging into the soil, preparing it for the new plants I had just purchased. Listening to my music in pure happiness, a shadow came over my shoulder and I looked up. Nigel was standing there in an old T-shirt; the sleeves had been cut off to the shoulders. I noticed how his upper arms looked so firm and tight around the muscles. His green eyes were looking at me intensely, and he had the biggest grin on his face.

"Oh, good grief! You caught me by surprise!" I said while standing up. He grabbed my arm to help me up and said, "You're really going to town around here. I love the fact that you are keeping your house up. That is so much better than some of the houses on this street. It's nice to have another homeowner in the neighborhood that cares about their property."

"I love it that you are a person like me that puts things in order," I said. "Not only that, you are a lovely redhead— vivacious and energetic." I was thinking, *Flattery might get you everywhere!* My mind was spinning a little,, and then I recognized what I was wearing. It wasn't the most flattering of outfits.

I changed the subject. "Nigel, do you remember that you said you would help me?"

He looked at me and said, "Of course! What do you need help with? Perhaps we can look at it and resolve it."

"Okay, follow me to the backyard. I have been cleaning my

gutters of leaves, but I have a couple of plastic sheets that I want to put on top my awning over my screen door so that when it rains, at least there will be a dry spot near the door for my cats." I motioned to him as I walked toward the back of my house, and I noticed that he was bouncing in his walk and smiling widely.

We got a ladder and placed it near my awning. I handed the large, cut sheets of clear plastic up to him, and he was happily placing them on top of the white plastic lattice work that the previous owners had left at the house. He said, "Let's see if these fit. Sure enough, there are a few nails in the way. If you have a hammer I can use to tap them in, I think these will work quite well for your cats."

I ran to get a hammer and handed it up to him. He was smiling down at me. When he was through, he climbed down the ladder and put it away for me in the garage. I then asked him to show me how to set the drip irrigation system and the water timer, and he proceeded to give me lessons on how he set his. This was encouraging! I was feeling an immense lifting of responsibility once I was shown a few tips on making things work.

It was a beautiful Fall day, so I said, "Nigel, would you like a glass of wine or a beer? I'd like to thank you very much for your help." He said emphatically, "It was my pleasure to help you. I like keeping things warm and friendly with my neighbors. Maybe I will take you up on the beer."

I said, "I'll go get you one and pour myself a glass of wine. We can sit out here on the patio and visit."

When I got back, he was checking out the water lines for the drip irrigation system. He had taken off his T-shirt and put it over one of the patio chairs. Definitely a man who likes to display his wares! We sat down and talked some more. My cat was nosing him, coming up to him. He gently reached down and started talking sweetly to him. Watching him, I couldn't help but notice how both of my cats really liked him.

We continued to talk, and the discussion turned to people in our lives. I told him that I was enjoying a new phase in my life. I shared with him that the difference in my life compared to what it was before was significant. We both admired the fact that we had careers and were now enjoying retirement, and with good health and energy that we didn't have before. I stood up to grab his T-shirt because my cat was licking the armpits. "Sneakers!" I said. "You stop doing that. What kind of sick kitty are you?" I handed the T-shirt back to Nigel, and he was amused at my admonishment of my cat.

He said, "You know, it would be fun to see *you* do that to my armpit!" Maybe it was the wine, maybe it was the influence of the discussion of a carefree life, but he stood up and took me in his arms. It wasn't a movement of passion, but it was an all-encompassing hold and felt so good. He then murmured in my ear, "You are such an attractive, beautiful woman. I am so lucky you have moved into this neighborhood."

I reached up and kissed him. After that kiss, I led him into my house to my bedroom. Was this an opportunity of sharing or an opportunity of physical awareness? Was this something very casual? I loved the feeling of how organic our intentions were. I wasn't sure what happened, but it was an afternoon of fun and exploring. He was a passionate and considerate lover. I felt like an indulgent princess being explored and loved all at the same time.

Afterward, as he held me in his arms, he murmured the nicest things that nuzzling could provide—sweet words of admiration and gratitude. This definitely felt good!

> *For women the best aphrodisiacs are words. The G-spot is in the ears. He who looks for it below there is wasting his time.*
> *—Isabel Allende*

CHAPTER 23

The Naughty Lady

Since my visit with Nigel that Thursday afternoon started going into the night, I decided that dancing that night could wait another week. After all, I could drive down to Badabing's for a great night of dancing on Friday.

I went that night with a full shot of "I'm too sexy for my shoes" attitude. I walked right into the club, walked up to the bar, and ordered a straight shot of Patron silver—straight up and no lime. I was feeling like Samantha from *Sex in the City*. It seemed that I could handle my liquor with that simple drink. If I drink any of the sugary drinks, then somehow I would get drunk. But the simple, straight drink loosened me up to dance and enjoy the music. The place was hopping. The energy from everyone in the place was sparking. I felt so alive! I was amazed at myself, walking into this place with such confidence, when less than a year ago I felt like a fledgling bird going in there.

I was asked to dance by so many men that it was intoxicating.

I felt like there must have been some kind of aura around me that said, "Pick me! Pick me!" I was amazed at my friskiness. For the next three days, my energy level and my vibration of living seemed so lively. On Tuesday, I was working in front of my house again, and Nigel saw me and came right over. He gave me the biggest hug and a kiss right out on the street. It's funny, but I looked around to see if anyone saw it. I could tell he hoped that someone would. What is it with public displays of affection? Men!

Well, he asked me over to his house for a tour. I told him that I wanted to close up my garage and lock my door, and then I followed him over. He invited me to see his upstairs, and before we knew it, we were frolicking on his bed. I could feel the pills of his old cotton sheets. There were many examples of a bachelor living frugally throughout his house. He had a fantastic stereo with nice soul music going. He house was fastidiously neat like the front and the back of the outside, but the sheets! When I would roll over, I could feel the abrasiveness of them. They were cheap cotton and had pilling all over them, but they were clean.

I commented, "Nigel, you need to replace these sheets if you're entertaining women up here." He replied nonchalantly, "I've never had anyone tell me that before." I apologized to him profusely, concerned that I had come off a bit fussy. Then I realized—of course! This man probably has a bevy of ladies coming through here. I told him I had several sets of sheets and that I was going to give some to him once I got into the boxes in my garage.

I didn't want to seem too intrusive, but I did ask him, "Do you entertain very often, Nigel?" He laughed and said, "Well, what do you define as *often*? You might be asking the wrong question, but I'll be honest, I do have two or three 'friends' in my life. I'm not a monk." After that, I realized I could not be hypocritical or I would be defining myself as a woman with an agenda.

I then told him, "Nigel, you know that I have been with only a few men since Larry died. I will tell you that this experience in my sexuality is all fairly new to me. I am finding that I do enjoy a certain freedom. I don't believe I'll ever settle down with someone again, but this freedom is truly exhilarating." He hugged me and said, "Lori, I'm so glad that you are a neighbor and now a good friend. I understand your caution and will respect that. Now, let me take a look at the *hootchie!*"

Later that evening, when it was dark, Nigel walked me across the street hand in hand to my front door. He then kissed me before I went in. When I closed the door, I had this feeling of youth and rejuvenation. There I was, fifty-eight years old, being naughty with a neighbor! Sassy, independent,, healthy, and naughty. Now I could call myself the naughty lady of Shady Lane.

The following Thursday, after doing more nesting in my home, I hopped into the shower, fussed myself into a frenzy, and decided to go to the Hilton in Pleasanton for the Hot Sizzling Summer Nights danceathon. I had last seen Frank there a few weeks before. While driving down, I was planning my words carefully so I could easily let him down from any expectations of a hookup. I felt I had enough men on my menu and didn't think Frank should be an additional item.

I walked into the outside pool area and looked around at all the familiar faces I had not seen for several weeks. The live music was moving people out on the dance floor. I walked over to the bar to get my normal shot of silver patron. Walt, one of Frank's normal hanging-out friends, was there at the bar. He turned around and saw me, and he immediately grabbed my hand. "Oh, I'm so glad you are here!" he said. I asked for my drink, and he said, "Make it a double because you're not going to like what I have to tell you." I looked at his face; he definitely had been crying.

I said, "What is it?"

He replied, "They found Frank dead last Sunday!"

"What?" My heart just sank to my stomach.

"Frank's daughter found him dead on her couch. You know, of course, he was living with her, didn't you?"

Frank had told me all about it that night at my house. My mind was going crazy with this news. It was spinning in all kinds of directions. *Do I have some kind of voodoo hex on men? Did I cause this? No, I didn't. Yes, I did!*

Then I asked Walt, "Did they say what the cause was?"

"They think it was a heart attack," he answered. *(Broken heart? Oh, please!* Why was my mind bending into all these directions?)

I took the double patron and chugged it down. Several of us talked about Frank throughout the night. Walt had known him the longest. Joe, the bartender, commented that Frank had been coming to the Hot Sizzling Nights there at the Hilton for almost ten years. He was a regular, and everyone knew him well. We all held our glasses up in honor of Frank and toasted to his life. Someone said, "Frank is riding his motorcycle now, faster than a speeding bullet with a big grin on his face!"

The rest of that evening was not the same for me. I kept thinking about what a nice person he was, honest and refreshingly sweet. His invitation for me to ride on the back of his Harley reminded me of how silly I would have looked wearing leathers and straddled on the back with my arms around him. I laughed about the visual and reminded myself again that life is way too short to not have fun.

> *To let life happen to you is irresponsible.*
> *To create your day is your divine right.*
> —*Ramtha*

CHAPTER 24

Spirituality in Progress

Two days later, Chris drove out to my house. It was Halloween, and we had made plans that I would ride with him to his gig. I dressed up in my outfit, complete with leopard ears, a choker, and a tail. It was so cold outside that I knew wearing something "sexy" would also mean being cold, so I changed it up. He still loved it and made comments on it.

We had a light dinner before we left, and I told him about Frank's death. He just blinked at me, absorbing the information. Chris had become a great lover, but he didn't want to be the only one in my life. His commitment level as a partner was very low, and he pounced on that topic often. I had told him about Frank before I took my previous drive up to the ranch, and he had teased me about becoming a naughty lady. He prided himself on being open and direct when it came to a person's sexuality. He was a man who was very uninhibited and proud of it. He believed that women, just like men, should be free to be with whomever they wanted.

I fussed about that image in the beginning, but he encouraged me to enjoy myself and to not hold back my opportunities. I kept putting into my mind, *He's not normal. He is saying these things because he doesn't want to be locked into any committed relationship.*

I told him how guilty I felt and that he should be careful about being a partner of mine. He smiled at me and said, "If your universe and/or my guru believes that will happen, then I welcome it when it comes. In the meantime, I'm having fun!"

I also filled him in on my liaisons with Nigel, and he just looked at me with amazement. "Lori, you are expanding into a well-rounded woman, and I find it very attractive. Keep it up, girl! I *love* it!"

We went to the gig in the Sacramento Valley near Elk Grove. It was a private Halloween party—very cold, but I enjoyed the opportunity to see him perform the three sets. He was a true musician through and through. I watched him playing his drums and dropping the taps and the bass drum beats in the right places. The band was a Country band and he absolutely loved performing. It was all over his face. He was in a zone of bliss.

During breaks, he would come over and hug me and kiss me in front of everyone. He was flirtatious, showing lots of public displays of affection.

He spent the night with me after the gig. We had a beautiful Sunday morning wake up with the sun and the Sunday paper, which I enjoy immensely. I felt maybe this was an opportunity to break the news to him about me going to the intensive, but then I hesitated. I sensed I needed to wait until the last minute to tell him. I could tell that he would get overexcited about my doing that, and I really wanted to experience it on my own without any influences. I realized that I needed to tell him because he lived one block away from the ashram and would very likely see me there.

Instead, I talked about how I was thinking about renting out the room in the front of the house. "It just doesn't make sense that it stays empty," I explained. "When I was talking to Nigel about it, he even mentioned that he could rent his whole house out and then rent out this room from me."

Chris looked at me with an intensity that I had not seen before. He said, "Well, there is probably someone out there who you can rent it to. I might even think about it." I told him, "We discussed that option for you when I was living in Dublin. Chris, if you think that moving in here could help you through your tough time right now, then I most warmly would offer it to you. You don't have to give me an answer now. Just think about it."

When he went out the door, he gave me a very warm embrace and a look of admiration over his shoulder. Did I sense a warm and fuzzy connection? Not from the tough Bronx, spiritually conflicted person I had gotten to know but a person who seemed to be softening around the edges. I had finally gone to see him perform. Maybe he felt some validation from someone in his life that he is a professional musician. He had mentioned to me that none of his friends from the ashram whom he had known for ages had ever made it to one of his performances. Maybe I got some brownie points there, who knows?

In the middle of the week, I started to feel feverish. I wasn't feeling well. I felt a kind of pressure in my lower abdomen. When I would pee, I had a burning sensation. *Oh, great! Now what have you gone and done?* It felt like another bladder infection coming on. When Chris and I had first started our relationship, I got one. The doctor had told me then that because I had not had sex in a long time, it was a typical reaction and a common problem.

On Thursday evening, I called Chris and touched base with him. I said, "Chris, you might see me over there at the ashram on Saturday."

"Oh? Why are you coming over here?" he asked

"Well, I signed up for the intensive that is being given. You had mentioned it many months ago, and now that I have settled into my house and with your introduction to Siddha Yoga, I thought maybe I would try this out."

There was a pause, and then he sounded excited about it. "I'm so glad you are doing that! I'm impressed that you are open to spirituality options. I think you'll like the people and the process. Maybe you'll get Shaktipat! Oh, I hope you do."

"Well, I didn't tell you earlier because I wasn't sure how you would react, but I just wanted to let you know just in case you are wandering around there."

He said, "Well, you just go in there with an open mind and enjoy your experience. We'll talk about it afterward."

Then I said, "If I see you there, do you want me to pretend I don't know you?"

Amazingly, he replied, "I think that might be a good idea."

It was a short and sweet phone call. I think I surprised him.

The next day, he called. He said, "Hi, this is Chris." *(Uh, I see your phone number on my display!)* "I was talking to my roommate here, and she and I talked about you attending. I wanted to make sure you understand what you might be getting yourself into. First, I think it is awesome that you are attending. I won't be there and will purposely stay away so you can get a full understanding of what you might experience. I know that this is an important experience and an expensive workshop. So enjoy yourself and don't worry about running into me. We can get together afterward and you can share your thoughts."

Well, now, this was a surprise! I replied, a bit amused, "Chris, thank you for your encouragement. I will look for you outside the ashram where we can meet up. Perhaps we can go eat dinner somewhere in Berkeley and talk afterward."

"That sounds like a plan to me. Make sure you wear clothes that aren't too revealing. The ashram is a place for modesty and contemplation. Enjoy yourself, and I'll see you after the intensive. Bye."

With that, I knew I had made a smart move in not telling him about it until the last minute. I liked this man, but he had intensity and passion about everything he likes, especially about his spirituality. Sometimes it got in the way of my understanding him. I guess it could be his Italian, Bronx intensity. But maybe it was just that this spirituality awareness was so very new to me.

That Saturday morning, I still wasn't feeling better and knew I was running a low fever. I went to the intensive anyway. I showed up in a modest outfit and signed in. The people there greeted me with a warm welcome and escorted me and several others into their shoe closet. We had to take off our shoes before entering into the meditation chamber. When I entered, I found that it was very peaceful with many pictures of the gurus on the wall. The lineage was respectfully placed on each of the three main walls. In front of the picture of the current guru were finely dressed women in Indian clothes, placing flowers in front of the portrait silently bowing their heads in respect. I looked at the guru's picture; she was beautiful, and her eyes beamed into the hall.

I looked around for a good place to sit. The options were a sitting pillow or a regular chair. I chose a chair that had a pillow in front of it, giving me the comfort of either. People were starting to drift in, finding their spots on the floor in front.

During the intensive, beautiful music played with words being displayed on the TV monitor up front. The swami gave us a warm welcome speech and gave the newest seekers an idea of what was going to happen. It was not a mystery. It reminded me so much of the many churches I had been to as a young person. They, too, had their symbols and different interpretations of God, source, or spirit. This path was really no different than going to a Catholic church or a synagogue. They all had their deities and symbols; I could see why so many would love that. I was raised a plain old Presbyterian. Not enough flare in that kind of religion.

The longest meditation lasted 45 minutes. I could feel my energy and focus of silence warming me inside, or was it the bladder infection? *I've got to schedule an appointment with the doctor on Monday,* I thought. My mind was wandering all over the place. Occasionally I was able to focus in the silence. I even saw the blue light.

I had been practicing meditation daily now for over a year. It was always an effort to keep my mind still. The peace and quiet in the meditation hall really helped me to finally put the noise in my brain to rest. I understand why so many people are drawn to meditation. I couldn't quite sing out the chants because I felt very uncomfortable expressing words that were unfamiliar to me. The ability to let loose was tightly bound up in me when it came to love. That's what these people were experiencing.

People were holding their hands in the air with euphoria. It reminded me of what I used to see at the Baptist church congregations with those who couldn't hold back "God" in their lives. Was the energy they felt moving them so much that they could express themselves so freely? I felt like an anvil, fixed to the ground, with my arms being held down. I could see why people love the freedom of expressing their devotion.

At the lunch break, they gave us an hour to mingle in the cafeteria. I'm a cautiously friendly person, and I did find three women to sit down with to enjoy the meal. I introduced myself and said that this was my first time there. All three of them were regulars. One, a practicing attorney, explained that she only came to the intensive each year to get a "refresher" on her spirituality. I noticed the people working behind the counters. They were all devotees of the ashram and had volunteered to do "seva"—a Sanskrit word for *service*—every day for breakfast and lunch and special events. There was Chris!

He walked by hurriedly, carrying a box of bottled water. He went over near our table to stock the refrigerator. I was amused at how he avoided eye contact with me. I chuckled, and two of the ladies glanced at me. They asked me if I knew anyone here, and I said no. "Did you enjoy the intensive so far?" they asked. I mumbled something to them; I was still enjoying Chris's quick and indirect moves, pretending to be "unrecognized." It seemed he was scoping something out in the small cafeteria. So much for not being in the way!

After the second session and a shorter meditation session with wonderful chanting, the Swami gave us our mantra, a unique set of words that went with "Om", part of the Guru's lineage. Then the intensive finally ended– none too soon. I knew I had some kind of infection and had to get to the bathroom really fast. I ran into the shoe room, found my shoes and headed towards the restroom. When I came out, I turned to go out into the lobby and into the gift store on the immediate right. The Swami was there and asked me how I had enjoyed the intensive. I offered the polite compliment and explored the store, buying a book on the guru and a meditation CD and then went out of the store. Chris was right there waiting for me as I moved towards the door. "How did you like the intensive?" he said in an excited voice.

"Oh, hi, Chris. I didn't think you would be here, but walk with me out the door." As we walked toward the door, several people stopped Chris, and he was obliged to politely introduce me to them. Was he hiding me from them? It felt strange to pretend I was only a brief acquaintance.

When we got out the door, he started asking me all kinds of questions. "Did you get into silence? Did you feel energy? How did you feel about the chanting?" I was walking toward my car. At that point I was physically feeling bad, and it had been a long day.

"Chris, it was interesting." I said it in an abrupt manner, but I wasn't feeling good. "It was something I could apply if I went to any church or synagogue. The people are welcoming, and the symbolisms with the mantras are perfect for the setting, but it isn't something I would wear on my sleeve. I don't do that."

He stopped me with a cautionary hold on my arm. "You didn't like it?"

I stopped on the sidewalk and said to him, "I did. It was a great experience. I didn't see any bright lights, flashes of intoxication. I didn't get enlightenment, and I understand why people are drawn to an active role of praying. I'm not sure this is what I'm seeking. I know that there is a wonderful power out there. It seems that we are all seeking it but in various ways. That is it."

He took his hand off my arm and continued to walk me across the busy street to my car. I asked him if he wanted to go eat somewhere, and he hopped in my car.

It had been months since we had really gone out together. This guy just didn't date. I had a hunch that with his frugality and very simple way of living, going out on dates had really never become a part of his life. He gave me directions to a great restaurant, and we had healthy food cooked by a local restaurant owner. The food was fresh and truly sublime. We continued to talk about my experience in the intensive. After dinner, I drove him to the house where he roomed and dropped him off. I wanted to get home. I was tired and still achy from whatever seemed to be bothering me.

On Monday, I called my doctor and scheduled a visit that day. I especially asked to speak to a nurse for advice on the phone, and she got me into the gynecology department. It was very likely a bladder infection, she said, but they wanted to double check.

I met the doctor, and she asked a series of questions. One of them was, "Have you had unprotected sex in the last year?"

I said, "Yes."

She stopped. "Are you married?"

I said, "No, I'm a widow."

She looked at me with amazement. I couldn't tell if it was my age she was reacting to or if she was judging me, but I could tell the wheels in her head were moving in fast speed. "You know about using condoms, don't you?"

I then explained, "I have had protected sex with several of my partners, except one, the first one I was ever with after my husband. I never had symptoms or problems. He assured me that he was safe. All the other partners were protected."

She again looked at me, amazed. I felt I had to explain to her like a daughter to a mother, but then I felt like a little girl who had been caught doing something nasty and had a quick sense of shame. I pushed that thought aside and started to get a little excited. "I know, it's amazing that at my age I am sexually active and that I am in this predicament, but it's probably just a bladder infection. I had one about a year ago."

She calmed me down and said, "Perhaps we need to do a few more tests regarding syphilis, gonorrhea, AIDS, and herpes." *Panic!* "So I would like to have you disrobe, and I will take some cultures." The monkeys in my brain were screeching by the time she got to the word *cultures.* I was panicking, something I hadn't felt in over two years. I was freaking out, very similar to driving on the Bay Bridge that day with Larry when he tried to step out.

Well, the outcome of that visit grounded me. I did have a bladder infection *and* very likely HSV-1, better known as herpes simplex virus-1oral. I had to wait until the results were mailed to me, but I walked out of the office with a prescription in hand and the monkeys flying out my ears. *Oh, my God! What have I done to myself? What it this a symbol of? You are such a slut! You have been such a bad girl. Now you have to* tell *everyone you have been with for the last five weeks that they have to be tested!* I literally counted on my hands who and what and when and where. I could count three recent possibilities. *Slut!*

I got home, took the antibiotics, took the HSV medicine, and got on the Internet. I Googled every website there was about herpes. There was even a support group and a dating site for people with herpes. *Good grief! How could I get HSV in my nether regions?* Well, you guessed it. Condoms work fine, but when the partner decides to become active in that area that pleasures you in other ways ... Who would have thought you could be that susceptible (or ignorant)?

I called my best and dearest girlfriend, who had told me years ago that she had contracted herpes from a trip to the hospital. I looked up that possibility, and what did I find? Forty percent of Americans have this virus and don't know they have it. That many of us contract it as small children, and five hundred thousand cases are diagnosed each year. I started thinking about the safety of having a single partner. *Whew!*

After my phone conversation with her, in which she told me that this is common, I knew it was still my responsibility to contact all my partners from the previous five weeks.

First on the list was Chris. "Hi, Chris. I was just diagnosed with HSV-1. Do you have it?" Sounds like a great way to greet someone on the phone. He took it in stride. I asked him to go to the men's health clinic and get tested just in case. He laughed at me; my voice must have been panicky. He assured me that he would.

Now Nigel needed to be contacted. I called him. "Hi, Nigel. Are you home?" "Why, yes, my lovely redheaded neighbor. Come on over!" I walked over to his house, gave him a big hug, and told him that I had some information he needed ASAP. He frowned when those words rolled off my tongue. "Nigel, I know you and I have been protected, but just in case, you need to get to your doctor and be tested for herpes."

He looked at me with wonderment, but I didn't see shock there. "Of course, I will. Whatever you think I need to do. I will do that tomorrow. Do you want to stay and visit?"

I wasn't in any mood for romance and told him that my body was still working on the medicines that the doctor had given me. We could get together in the future, but I needed to get back to my house.

When I got home, I immediately took a deep breath. Is it silly to panic? The universe is definitely telling me something: *Lori, slow down in your physical pursuits. You are having way too much fun, and you need to take a breath.* Oh, I've got the message loud and clear!

Well, I don't have to call Frank, I thought. *He's dead. What in the world did he die from?* My mind started to panic again. I sat down in front of my computer and decided to google the word herpes again.

> **Slow down and enjoy life. It's not only the scenery you miss by going too fast; you also miss the sense of where you are going and why.**   **—Eddie Cantor**

CHAPTER 25

Thanksgiving Is for Coming Home

Chris called me the following day and told me he went to take the tests. He said his results would be ready in about a week. He said he wanted to come by in a couple of days and asked if I would be around for his company. I told him to come on over and visit. I loved his company and would love to see him.

When he got to my house, his demeanor was different. He seemed more intense, maybe a bit anxious. At first I thought, *Uh-oh, this is bad news! This means he has some serious disease!* I broached the subject quickly and effortlessly.

"So, are you here to tell me the results of your test?" I asked simply.

He replied with a quick smile. "Oh, I went to the men's health clinic and waited for testing. The end result—I have nothing in me that could have resulted in your outbreak."

I looked at him in amazement because I was still in denial that this had happened to me and wanted someone to blame for this. My mind was saying, *It isn't him because you would have had symptoms way before this.* I looked at him. This man was one of the most honest and present people I had ever known. He looked at everything directly and would comment about it as it was. I knew in my mind and heart that he would not be a liar or a deceiver in any way.

I calmed down, and we hugged each other in a comforting way. He said, "Lori, this all happened for a reason, and you'll figure it out someday, so I just want to hold you for a moment." Then he smiled at me and teased, "You probably got *shaktiputz* from the intensive at the ashram!" It seemed that his humor was always perfectly timed for moments like this. We stood in my kitchen hugging in a comforting solid connection that I hadn't felt in a very, very long time.

I then sat on one of my kitchen stools, and he said, "I know that you are looking for a roommate, and you did offer me your extra bedroom. I think I would like to take you up on your offer."

I hesitated for a moment and then realized that this was a turning point in my life and probably his as well. I said, "Chris, I would be delighted if you occupied that room. I know that you don't have much money coming in right now, but perhaps we can work out a deal where you buy all the food, as an 'in lieu of' arrangement."

He smiled at me with a big smile of relief. "I'm really a quiet person on a day-to-day basis. I could move in right after Thanksgiving because the current roommate situation is getting tense." He then explained the characters of his other roommates. All of them were women who were devotees of his guru. They were older than him, and he got along well with most of them, but one of them was getting testy about his day to do laundry. I laughed out loud because it sounded so juvenile that people in their late fifties and sixties were complaining to each other about their laundry days.

I told him, "Chris, then why don't you give your notice to them that you will be moving out at Thanksgiving. We can work out some way of moving your items here in my car." He didn't have much; this guy lived very simply. All he had was a mattress on the floor and many boxes with clothes, books, and pictures in them. The only other large items were the pieces of his drum set, which he could fit in his small compact car.

We both seemed relieved, even a bit jubilant about this decision. Every other day, he would come out and bring a few boxes to put in his new room. We would share our events of the day, make love, eat simple foods, and just laugh. When I handed him a key to the house, he smiled at me and said, "Oh, goody!" like a little boy.

On Thanksgiving Day, I drove over to his residence in Oakland. Most of the homes in that neighborhood were shared homes for many of the devotees like a commune. We loaded his twin mattress into my car and then drove to another Thanksgiving family get-together on the peninsula. We both reflected on the fact that this was our second Thanksgiving together.

My son, his wife, and my granddaughters were there. I had not seen them for about a month. My son and daughter knew before-hand that Chris was moving in with me. My son told me, "I know you're happy, Mom, and that really is all that counts." I enjoyed being with my granddaughters, who were growing so fast.

We both enjoyed the gathering, knowing that once we drove home, it would be to a home that we would share together. Chris called his parents on our drive and informed his parents about his move. He told his parents in his own eclectic sense of humor, "Mom, Lori went to a Thanksgiving dinner and she is bringing home the turkey!"

> *Forever on Thanksgiving Day, the heart will find the pathway home.* —*Wilbur D. Nesbit*

CHAPTER 26

Problem Solving My Intention

After Chris moved in, we started getting into a routine. Every morning after breakfast, I would always meditate. I felt stronger and more centered after a forty-five-minute process of reflection. Chris shared many of his books on spirituality, and I shared with him my accumulation of self-help books. We put them on the bookshelves together, realizing that they were truly part of our abundance and a path that we were traveling together.

Life got happier for me; he was constantly coming into my room to see what I was doing. He would be busy talking and telling me stories that he had never shared before, I would share silly stories of comparison with him, and we became wonderful friends. The art of lovemaking became one of the elements of wonderful surprise. We were acting like two teenagers.

About a week after Chris moved in, the weather got colder. In the middle of the night, there was a clanging moving throughout my house. I could tell it was the water pipes. The next morning,

I got on the internet to search a solution. With the prescribed diagnosis that there was air in my pipes, I followed the instructions of closing down the all the faucets and valves from the back of the house to the front. Then opening up the faucets and letting the water run full force for five minutes. It seemed to work for about two days.

Another night of clanging pipes, and I was starting to get frustrated. I had been in the house for almost three months and had not had these problems before. Incensed, I followed all the motions of shutting down the valves and then turn them all back on again. The clanging stopped.

Then two days later it came back with a vengeance. This time, I went out into my garage and ranted "Larry, I know that you are doing this just to be funny. I'm tired of this, and I have done all the things that you would have done if you were there. Will you stop now?"

The pipes have not banged again. Was the universe or Larry's energy still around me making fun of my dilemma of being a fix-it queen? I think so.

I was looking forward to my cruise with my sister-in-law, Diana. The Abraham-Hicks cruise to Mexico with about four hundred other people would begin right after New Year's. I knew that being with these people would be so uplifting to me. To prepare myself, I often put in a video or an audio and listened after meditation. Chris was listening along with me and was starting to understand the messages of positivity. He was grasping where I was coming from and how thinking toward good helps you put forth intentions of acting and participate in higher vibration.

The nice benefit of having him in my house, other than the

"friends with benefits" arrangement, was that he would be the caretaker of my cats while I was gone. Life just got simpler.

While on the cruise with Diana, my understanding of the laws of attraction deepened. The fun of so many people sharing positivity was energizing. While on the cruise, the Abraham-Hicks collective said that they were planning an Australia/New Zealand cruise. My heart just sang! I talked about it so much to Diana, and she, in her own positivity process, was so supportive. I thought about ways to go on this cruise. I asked if she would she be my roommate, and she replied, "No, Lori, I really don't have any desire to go to Australia, but I'm sure you will find someone." I knew down deep that this was my trip of a lifetime.

Larry and I had talked many times about going there. It was the one thing that had been on our bucket list for many years. All hope went away when he got sick. After seeing how he handled traveling on our Mediterranean cruise, I lost all hope of doing this. In my heart, I decided I was going to go on this cruise and take the small amount of ashes I had of him with me to complete my journey with him.

After I got back from my Mexican cruise, I contemplated how I could financially manage the cruise. This was an undertaking. I had the costs of my Bay Area house and those of my ranch house. I was still making trips up occasionally to make sure it was taken care of, but the costs of electricity, propane, satellite (for TV and Internet), insurance, property taxes, and occasional maintenance were taking a big hit on my budget. But I was so fortunate that I didn't have a mortgage on it. After all, it was our retirement house. Yes, I splurged on the trip to Mexico, but I worked through my finances well. I talked to my girlfriend in the Bay Area who was a commercial property owner. "Lori," she said, "make your property work for you! If you aren't living in it and it is becoming a burden, then start earning money off it." This was sage advice from a woman who had struggled with raising her daughter as a single woman and now owned several commercial and residential pieces of property.

I took a trip up to the ranch and contemplated what to do. I definitely wanted to go on this trip, and here was an opportunity to bring in extra cash. I knew deep down that my children would be opposed to it. Over the last two years, my son had made three trips to the house, and my daughter had made about seven or eight. I talked about it with Diana at great length. The property that the house was on wasn't mine; it belonged to my father-in-law, Ray. There was an underlying agreement between all of his children that if they built their homes on the property (which was expansive), they wouldn't own the deed to the property; it would eventually go into a trust. But we all agreed that if we built our retirement homes there, we would be responsible for the costs of the building, permits, and supplemental property taxes. It worked.

As I reflected on my current situation and went over my pros and cons with Diana, I knew then and there how I was going to pursue this. So, upon that, I made the decision to rent the house. It would all work out—or so I thought!

I went back to my house in the Bay Area and prepared to carry out the decision I had made. I was so happy that I was going to Australia and New Zealand. I asked Chris if he would like to join me. I knew the answer—this would be an extremely expensive trip for him—but I thought I'd ask him anyway.

Chris answered with the utmost sincerity, "Lori, I would love to travel with you. I am sure it would be fun. But I can't even take a trip to see my family because of my back. I truly need to heal and figure out how I'm going to work through my own problems. I'm absolutely sure there is a person—maybe even one of your dancing friends from Badabing's—who would love to join you. Now, wouldn't that be fun?"

Well, at that point, it was my intention to find a cruise roommate. I shared my news on Facebook with all of my friends, offering an opportunity to join me on the cruise. I had hoped one of them would respond. There were many "likes" on my status and a few comments from friends on how they would love to join me, but no offers to come with me.

It was a couple of days later when I received my son's e-mail. It took me a while to figure how I would respond to two very upset adult children. I knew that this was very common when a parent dies. I saw other widows and widowers dealing with their children's withdrawals from two-parent consistency.

As I smoothed the fleecy, soft, warm sheets on my bed, flipping the cover back, I tri-folded the white comforter at the bottom of the bed. I realized that for the first time in over two years, I had a sense of relief. Relief that I was no longer obligated to answer to anyone but myself.

Relief that I could choose to do anything I wanted to do that day or any day without requiring validation from someone else. I opened my patio door and took a big breath of the cool breeze that came through. I walked out onto the patio and sat and listened.

I heard the birds chirping over my bird feeders. The hummingbirds that I had fondly fed from the feeder were buzzing back and forth, filling up the six small perches on the feeder. I realized that I felt like those birds. They were flying around from tree to bird feeder, chirping with gratitude that someone had provided them with food. I realized that I was free to fly.

This was a lifting of responsibility, that of having to be the dutiful, planned, focused person I had been for decades. I smiled at the scene in front of me and looked up into the sky with gratitude. "Thank you," I said to the universe. "I needed that!" I walked over to my computer to compose my answer to my children's horrible e-mails.

I sent my first e-mail to Diana as a follow-up confirmation that it was okay by my father-in-law Ray, to rent my house. She wrote back, and I forwarded it onto my children letting them know that this wasn't just a flighty decision on my part.

> Dear Donné and Dan,
> Please read the following:
> **From:** Diana Anzini
> **To:** Lori Anzini
> **Subject:** Re: Rental of the house
>
> Dear Lori, I've read your letter to Grandpa and he said, "Just tell Lori to go ahead and rent it. It's fine with me. Tell the kids that they can stay with us whenever they want to." In fact, if they will let me know ahead of time I will plan a getaway and they can have the whole house. This will always be one of their homes and they are always welcome here. Hugs to all, Diana

I hope the e-mail from your Aunt Diana calms your fears of what I am doing. Contrary to stories that you have been hearing ... the Anzini family supports me in doing this.

I love you both and always will. If you choose to remove me from your lives, that is your choice. Both of you have told me that you can't stand the person that I have become. I'm sorry for that, but as you will understand in time, I need to do things that make me happy. I could give you a short list of things that don't make me happy ... and that would be both of you making conditions on what I do with my life. I believe that you may not understand this statement in your child's mind because you react to it as a child ... (you are both my children, and that will never change).

But if you truly understand me, you would support me in my decisions, whatever they are, and not make emotional statements about me not seeing you or your families ever again. You should understand me in your beautiful Adult minds and should be happy that your mother is making an independent and happy life for herself. I've grown in areas of thought and clarity that are meaningful to me. I have the ability to understand that to truly be happy, I must love myself. I am taking care of my health; I am physically in better shape now than I have been for over 25 years. All of my old friends have noticed this and love the glow that I carry with me. I reflect on my abundance and thank the universe every morning with gratitude. I remember how my mother changed after my dad passed away ... I worried that she would wither and become despondent, and was I wrong. For more than 10 years, she settled into doing things that she really liked to do, until her health failed ... her life as an independent woman went on. And we loved her for it. I raised two very independent and opinionated children, on purpose. I appreciate that you have concerns, but please realize, that it is unnecessary.

I am very happy with my new friends in my life, and there are many. You both have made mention about my friend Chris. You have made innuendos about it in the beginning and now it has become more evident that you don't like him. Let me be clear. He is just a best friend who lives with me. He celebrates the fact that I go wherever I want, whenever I want, and hang out with whomever I want to hang out with. He brings humor and laughter into my life. I believe that his visit in my life has a purpose, to make me understand myself and give me support when I doubt myself. I do the very same for him. We work well together in emotional support. Chris has nothing to do with my money or financial decisions.

Your concerns about my finances go unfounded. My decisions do not impact either of you. What I do, where I go, and how I go about it are truly my business, not yours. By making blanket statements about my partying around and living carefree without responsibility does not make a good relationship with me. I have tried to go past that, but you are both insistent in your cause ... to stop me from making a decision that would make me happy. That is unfortunate. If I want to do something including going on a cruise to have fun ... or just flying to Las Vegas ... that should not be a concern of yours.

You should rejoice in the fact that I am very happy in what I'm doing.

As I told you both ... renting the house out is a temporary situation. I am doing this until I can collect social security. I selected your cousin Emily primarily because I asked her about her concerns of me renting the house and she volunteered to find the right neighbor. She is impacted by who is selected as her neighbor. I believe that this is a good idea. She has a lot at stake in this. No, she isn't a real estate agent. I called a real estate agent in Garberville many weeks ago ... one that has done a lot of business with your grandfather and your aunt.. He talked to me about the rental market and gave Emily a list of people—at her request—that were looking for a rental. The list he gave her was cleared by him as great people that are looking for rentals. She also posted on Craigslist, carefully, and got over 30 requests, of which she weeded them all out carefully. Emily has been doing rentals for several years. She and Diana have experience in this with their own rental in Ferndale. She has resources that she can immediately use for any concerns. Her father-in-law has many rentals in Southern California and has given her lots of advice. Emily is quite pleased to do this and allowing her to do this creates harmony with the ranch family.

Emily has been very supportive with me. She has volunteered to do this for me. I will be paying her a small amount to be my property manager. This is good for her ... she will make a stipend for her work, and she will take care of any issues that will come up. She has many contacts and knows a lot of Southern Humboldt people. She has assured me that all will go well, and I am willing to trust her on this. Her length of living there near your grandfather on the ranch has great merit and I can rely on the fact that her relationship with your grandfather is excellent. Utmost ... he is the owner of all of the property. Family harmony is important to him.

Your grandfather is also excited about this. He is looking forward to having someone new to gossip about, including the "cute chick" that will be moving into the house. He has stated to me several times, that no house should just sit there and be unused. It's good for the house to be occupied and good for the neighbors, too. As for the couple that Emily has found for me ... they are professionals. They are 33 and 35 years old. She is the executive director of the senior center in Redway. He is a plumbing contractor. (Your grandfather is extremely pleased about this!). He may have knowledge on water systems that the ranch really needs assistance with. They do not have children ... but have two dogs. They LOVE to snowboard and go to Lake Tahoe when they have a chance. Your grandfather has even asked if Eric rides a horse.

I hope that the preceding statements will lessen your fears of what I'm doing. It's unfortunate that you both are upset about this. I'm sorry that you feel this way, but I can think of nothing else that would change your minds. We go around in circles when we talk about it ... and the emotional part on all of us is draining. My only offer to both of you is that I contact hospice or a family counselor and that we have a couple of sessions to help us move through this process. This opportunity may help all of us get around the issue that you believe your mom has changed and that you can't stand her. Stating that and then hanging up only hurts my process of being me. Both of you have removed me from your lives. Change happens, no matter what, but somehow I have embraced it and you have not. This saddens me that you have not supported me.

All my love that is always yours,

Mom

Whatever happens around you, don't take it personally ... Nothing other people do is because of you. It is because of themselves.
                                        —*Don Miguel Ruiz*

CHAPTER 27

Take a Deep Breath!

Days later, my son sent me a quick email notifying me that I was no longer invited to my granddaughter Clara's first birthday party. I didn't receive any more emails from them, so I more or less figured that this was going to be a standoff. I realized that they were hurt. But by their responses and reaction, it threw me back into a depression of monumental guilt. My mind went into overdrive. Chris was supportive, knowing my emotional state. He delicately reminded me that when people react to your decisions, it's usually their problem, not yours.

I went up to unload my house and move my furniture down to the Bay Area. I made a decision that sometimes a person just has too much stuff. Both Diana and Louise were there to help. My daughter went up two days before I got there and removed a few items. She unloaded her disappointment on her aunt Louise. She took with her the picture of my granddaughter, Haley; a beautiful bottle of tequila that I had purchased at the factory in Puerto Vallarta; and all of the family pictures that I had in a cupboard.

Louise, being a highly sensitive and dramatic person herself, provided the sounding board that my daughter needed. She helped me pack up items for storage and moving and told me about my daughter going through the house. She then told me, "Consider yourself 'spanked' by your kids."

Several weeks turned into months. I received no Mother's Day cards from either of my children. That was significant. I got that message; I felt the loss.

It didn't matter. I had made the decision and moved on with my life. I felt that this decision was worthy of my cause: to move on. The rest of the year, I had no contact with either of my children. They had blocked me from Facebook, and I couldn't see what they were doing. My daughter-in-law and her parents "unfriended" me on Facebook. I thought about the feelings I had about that and developed more and more resentment toward my children.

My closest and dearest friends knew what had happened, and I figured out that ranting about what "they did to me" just made it worse; it continued to create bad energy for me. They sympathized with me, offering various supporting opinions that what they were doing was unjust. Many explained that my children just thought that they were "entitled"—and why does this generation of children have this sense of entitlement? Then I finally realized that this was the universe sending me messages to begin a process of more growth and expansion. I saw it for what it was and tried to remove my reactionary mind from my children's criticism of me.

Chris and I continued our own growth in getting to know each other better spiritually. Being together on a day-to-day basis presented us with an opportunity to share our books, videos, and reflections with each other. This was a communication that I had never had with Larry. Chris and I had defined ourselves with being present. We became fond of Eckhart Tolle, Neale Donald Walsch, Gregg Braden, Deepak Chopra, and a bevy of other authors who resonated with us. Interesting enough, my practice in stillness made me happier.

I was looking forward to my cruise after New Year's. In October, my sister Karla called me to touch base with me and renew our sisterhood. She had disconnected from me when everything fell apart between my children and me. She got caught up in the drama, becoming another sounding board for my daughter and son. She stopped communicating with me because she instinctively knew that somehow, her connections with my children would get back to me. I understand that now.

After she finally contacted me, she would come and visit occasionally. She and I agreed that whatever was happening with my children, she wouldn't share information about what they were doing. We both agreed that my children needed to come to me and not pull her into a triangular family quagmire. We needed each other as sisters. It was too painful for me. At least she was back in my life.

We mutually agreed to fly down and be with my brother near Tucson, Arizona. He had just had a third of his liver removed because of Hepatitis C. He was our only brother, and we had not seen him since he had moved to Arizona. It was a remarkable reunion between the three of us. We, as grown-ups (ages sixty-four, fifty-nine, and fifty-six) had finally established a truce and could share all of our childhood blaming on our own realities—what our parents did to us or what we as individuals believed they did to us. We finally got past the "You did this to me" stage. Our maturity manifested in recognizing that whatever our experience was during our youth was really insignificant to our lives in the present. It was a beautiful, harmonious, and loving get-together. All three of us matured that Thanksgiving.

Just before Christmas, the feeling of abandonment from my children brought up an ugly dream. I don't dream like this unless it's meaningful, and it did present some significance and awareness. I tried to read between the lines of its meaning, but when I woke up I had the urge to write it down.

December 6, 2010

I woke up this morning with a body ache that suggested that I worked very hard in this vivid dream. I rarely dream vividly, but I'm starting to understand that these dreams I have, do have meaning. The last two years, I have rarely dreamed ... but when I wake up remembering the dreams I understand now that the universe is really reminding me to do something ... and that is to take care of myself when reacting to the dream.

When I reflect on the actions of the dream ... the angst that I had was frightfully real. My son Dan was hosting Christmas dinner (or at least I think it was). I wasn't invited, I was spending Christmas on my own ... Chris may have been in the background, because I know someone was there but they were silent in my actions but were just THERE. I decided with determination that I was going to go to this dinner. The long walk was around an area very similar to being woodsy and near the ocean. The air was clean and crisp. I could hear sounds of seagulls and the distant sound of people's voices, as if they were on a beach. There was the Golden Gate Bridge there (or was it the Golden Gate?) ... it was a famous bridge because lots of people were on the edges of the cliffs with chairs, lounge chairs, picnics, and children. There was a city right next to it with many types of shops and markets leading from them to the cliff edges.

I was trying to get to my son's house, which I knew where it was from the view ... somewhere near the bridge. I stopped and watched someone barbecuing chicken on a huge barbecue. The chickens were spitted piece by piece on these large sticks, the barbecue sauce dripping into the fire causing the flames to roar. It smelled so nice that I decided to buy one of the sticks full of chickens to take to his house. I was walking the full distance to his house. I had not driven in a car in the whole dream. I was carrying this big stick to his house which was steps away.

I walked in without knocking, because the door was open, but there were no cars in front of the house and the garage door was open with no cars in it. I walked down a hallway and saw the back of my son working in his kitchen. I came in with the chicken. There was no warm greeting. I told him that I brought chicken to add to the dinner. He turned around and said to me "I wish you hadn't, Rich and Linda are out right now bringing the turkey here. We have plenty, but just put it down on the counter." I looked around, the house was absent of all people. His wife Natalie and the babies weren't there in the house either. I assumed that she was with the babies with her mother and father. My son picked up a cell phone and starting texting, not talking to me, but concentrating on his cell phone. I asked him while walking around the house, "Is Donné coming?" He absently told me while focused on the cell phone "Yes." It was as if I didn't exist in his life; perhaps I was just a ghost to him.

I decided to walk out of the house and just go back to where I started on this trip ... wherever it was it was across from the bridge on the other side and there were all kinds of obstacles to hurtle over. I was walking away from the whole situation not confronting the absence of emotion I felt from my son. His absence of love and acknowledgement that I was his mother was making me angrier each step I took. I tried taking a shortcut to my destination (wherever that was!). I turned to the left down a path, and it took me to these huge metal doors, green and weather stained. There were clothes hanging on the front of the doors on old hangers. The clothes looked old, worn, and stained ... as if they belonged to homeless people. There was a shopping cart to the right of the door. I opened the door and smelled urine in the cement tunnel walkway ... and bravely marched to the other side and opened the door on the other side.

When I opened the door, the pronounced cement step was like an overhang ... right to the cliff hanging over the ocean and the splashing waves below. The ocean waves were turquoise blue and vibrant, inviting me to jump right in and wash myself of the smell that I just walked through. Was this a metaphor? I looked intensely in the water above ready to jump in ... when I had this feeling of strength shoot through me. "Go back, confront the situation, remind him that you are his mother." I turned around. I marched through the smelly tunnel, through the metal door, and stepped onto the worn dirt path. I walked up to his house. There still were no cars, the doors were wide open, and I walked down the hallway toward the kitchen. I heard another voice, it was my daughter's. I stopped to listen. She was talking to him while he was texting on the phone. They did not see me and I heard her say, "Who brought the chicken?" He nonchalantly said, "Mom did." My daughter asked him, "What does Natalie think about that?" He put down his phone and looked right at her. "Natalie thinks Mom is losing it and should be committed. I think she is right!"

I didn't move and immediately turned around, marching back out of the house, back onto the path that I just had walked up. That's when I woke up from this dream.

My body was clenched, my hands gripped in fists. My shoulders were aching, and I had a feeling like I had just worked out in a major fight. As I lay in my bed in my soothing, soft, fleece sheets and thought about what I may have learned. I realized that the universe was telling me something, that perhaps I am making a big deal about this relationship with my kids. I felt like I had lost control of a relationship with the two most important people in my life. I gave birth to these people. My loss of them is as great as the loss of my husband. I had an understanding that these people, though they were my children, had really removed me from their lives, and I need to be aware that it's okay for them to do that.

Yes, it hurts, terribly, but along with that comes a bit of freedom that I need to recognize; I am not burdened with the requirement of being their mother anymore. And it's okay to feel this freedom because being their mother requires guilt and a performance of being a person that I no longer felt comfortable doing. It would require me to go into a pattern of behavior that I did not want to experience again—experience of responsibility, control, and an expectation to react the way I don't want to anymore. With that acknowledgment, I knew that my internal love was just around the corner—the *me* that is happiest.

Three days after Christmas, I left for my cruise to New Zealand and Australia. It was one of my most memorable days. I had planned for this for ten months. The cruise had matched me up with one of the Abraham-Hicks workshop attendees, so my worries were gone. She seemed like a lot of fun, and we had several phone conversations before the trip. We both seemed to be seeking joy. Her last name was Houdini and we just marveled over the phone on how synchronicity may have played a part in that. What were the odds of two women with the name of Anzini and Houdini being matched as roommates for a cruise of a life time?

Chris drove me to the airport. He was excited for me. He knew I had paid a lot emotionally for my trip. It was going to be a long trip over the ocean. I knew that I was heading for a magnificent experience. I brought some of Larry's ashes with me, with full intentions of dispersing them somewhere near the New Zealand fjords. The cruise ship was going to go into several of them. I had bought a lot of Internet time to keep my Facebook friends informed and up to date on what I was doing and how much this trip meant to me. My most spirited writing was an immediate response to how I felt one of those twelve days:

So I'm here on the Ship's internet—it's faster than my laptop in my cabin room. We are out of Milford Sound and going west to Hobart, Tasmania (Australia's little boot). Yes, there will be Tasmanian devils to be found! For those "Abrahamsters" out there, my closeness to source is amazing! There are about 800 of us on this ship sharing our thoughts and good vibrations! Life is truly sweet!

Yesterday was truly a wonderful day! The weather was absolutely stunning, and the ship went through the New Zealand Fjords (Dusky Sound, Doubtful Sound, and Milford Sound). This was an important day for me; you see, I took a little bit of Larry with me. He and I years ago discussed going on this exact cruise … but it wasn't meant to be. He LOVED the pictures he saw of the striking mountains and the beautiful clear and calm waters.

I started to pinch some of his ashes into Doubtful Sound, which those of you who knew Larry would have thought it appropriate. But the truth was, there were too many people on the top side … and I couldn't have been discreet.

By late afternoon we headed into Milford Sound, piloted by a Kiwi (New Zealander). He turned the ship around in the sound … everyone moved to the front and I stayed in the aft … it was PERFECT! He now has gone to New Zealand! I will post pictures later.

Today … on our way to Hobart … I spent the afternoon listening to the words of Abraham on the "laws of attraction." The art of relationships is truly so defined and simple … but those who come up to ask questions ask those questions from a feeling of a lack of something. That feeling is so real, I could relate. But as Abraham speaks (Esther Hicks) … they remind us that, it is truly all "irrelevant" because what we feel we lack isn't really so … it's just that we remove ourselves from a vibration that seems like we lack … when of course what we really have is abundance! (My interpretation … someone else probably heard it differently. But even that is irrelevant!)

Once I posted my musings, I knew that somewhere along this rocky path I journeyed, I had healed. It wasn't an easy path; it was one with misgivings, doubts, and self-recriminations. But I know that when we go through these upheavals, we become stronger and resilient.

I made wonderful new friends on this trip. One phenomenal woman, Vera, an Australian, and a funny, intelligent person who became my trip buddy and maybe a mentor. We shared much in common, we were both widows. Her insight and intuitive reasoning on why our paths can be so difficult is that we just get in our own way. It takes practice to realize this and being with someone else on the same social and emotional field helped lift me in many ways.

When ship landed in Sydney it docked right under the famous bridge, I couldn't help but recognize that maybe this had been a part of my dream. I had wonderful experiences with so many people on that cruise. All of us seeking happiness and joy during the trip. Vera had to catch a plane from Sydney to Adelaide where she lived. She had about eight hours to pass, so I volunteered my hotel room to stow her luggage until she needed to leave.

She became my tour guide that afternoon. We were both exhausted from the cruise…we were trying to get our land legs back. We headed over to the nearest coffee shop for the free internet and a caffeine fix to let our loved ones know we got to Sydney. We left and went back to my room and that's when I realized my wallet was missing.

After hurrying across the street to the coffee shop, a sweet cashier handed back to me my wallet, all cash and credit cards intact. My special medallion dropped on the boardwalk near the Sydney Opera house during our walk along the harbor. After a tasty lunch with Vera under the Opera House along the waterfront, we went running back and I retrieved it. It was lying right in front of an aborigine playing the didgeridoo. Thousands of people had walked across it in the 45 minutes that I had lost it. Three days later when I was home unpacking, I realized I had left all of my jewelry in a drawer in my hotel. With a distressed email and phone call to the hotel, I received ALL of it back within fifteen days, including my amulet with Larry's ashes in it. My vibrational pull was so positive that I lost nothing and gained everything on that trip.

My children were still boycotting me, but it wasn't as heartbreaking as before. Things seemed to be warming up, and I know that at some point, our differences will work out. I continue to send birthday cards to my children and their families. I continue to take the five-hour car trip up Highway 101 to visit the ranch house and visit with my in-laws, but not as often.

I also realize that I have great abundance, and it isn't necessarily material things. The abundance that I recognize is that we all have strength to get by. We are all truly seeking joy. So my tribute with this book is that I truly hope women and men who have lost their partners in life can take my experiences and know that whatever happens to them happens for a reason. You truly have no control over the path that is thrown in front of you, but you do have the responsibility to seize the moment, suck the deliciousness out of that creation, and enjoy it till you die.

Life is way too short to have angst about what should have been said and how it should have been said or how it was received. Everyone receives information that they think is valuable to them—or not—and react in a way that they are comfortable with. As I write this book, it is a reflection of the things that happened to me during and after Larry's illness and death.

I have now taken my experiences and put them on paper. I know others will take from my story the parts that they need to help their lives improve. If that happens, my intentions became truth and, for that, I am grateful. I have moved on, but you just don't move past a thirty-six-year marriage without looking back at it and rejoice with glee about the wonderful path you made with your life partner. Moving on? It means finding peace in your daily routine. It means happiness in knowing that you have experienced a beautiful love of someone so special that you made a life together. Love yourself and know that your partner is watching you, smiling at you, and wanting you to seek joy, not sadness!

> *How people appear in life is the predominant force on what they attract. I will wake up each morning with full appreciation of who I am and breathe in the beauty of what this universe has given me.*   —Lori Anzini

CHAPTER 28

A Soliloquy to My Appreciation of Living

The ocean smell is inviting me. I will never get the scent out of my memory. My life in the village of Mendocino was really so magical. I had a good mother and father, who settled their family in this area after so many years of traveling in the military. My early travels prepared me for the "stranger in town" presence and the ability to make friends with anyone. No, I wasn't related to anyone there in this small town, but the eventual welcoming of the community and the participation of my very community-minded parents will always be cherished in my mind.

I graduated from Mendocino High School, went away to business school in Sacramento, and created a life with purpose, but the experiences of that quaint coastal village will always linger in my heart and mind. Nothing will ever replace or could ever match that little village on the Pacific Ocean.

I look forward to the day—some day in the far, far-off future—that I will rest my weary body and settle amongst the waves off Heeser Drive as they crash around me, gently rocking me into bliss.

Prologue

During the writing of this book, I had many emotional inspirations that revealed my transformation. It's true that they say time does heal old wounds. Understanding this, I chose not to push myself into my children's lives or throw guilt trips at them about my loss of them. They, too, are still healing from the loss of a father.

As parents, we instinctively know how people will react to our actions. But somewhere in that process, when we know our actions are good for us, it isn't always seen as good for the ones we love most. Understanding this is fundamentally important for everyone in the family to heal.

My children and I love each other very much. My daughter and I are on our path of renewal in our love for each other. We just couldn't reach for each other without assistance. Ultimately, with the help of a family therapist and lessons on how to lovingly communicate with each other, it is much better now. We both understand where our love floundered. It is more unconditional now than it ever was.

My son and I eventually talked, and we agreed that the lack of communication created pain in our hearts and our minds. My 2011 reunion with my children and grand-daughters at Christmas was a healing event for all of us.

Relationships with our grown children are so important during grief. The process is painful. Some people have tried to relate with me with statements similar to "I've gone through a divorce, I know your loss." I keep my own comments to myself when this happens, aware that many people don't know how to communicate with you with such a loss. I'd like to say back "Yes, I share with you that we both have lost a marriage, but that isn't the same as a spouse, or partner dying. There is no comparison." But I don't. This is a common experience shared by widows and widowers everywhere. We've all been there.

Simply said, communications with our loved ones – the survivors of the loss - need to continue in order to balance ourselves; steadying our resolve from the shaky area of death and dying. It's tough trying to do it alone. Grief does not go away in three days, three months, or even three years. It hits you in the face at the most inopportune times, when you least expect it.

Once you realize what that feeling is, and you are aware of its meaning, the only thing you can do is just smile at it and let it go. What I have learned is that dealing with grief, I had to learn to love myself. Everything else is just a bonus!

> *Parents can only give good advice or put them on the right paths, but the final forming of a person's character lies in their own hands.*
> *—Anne Frank*

My Inspirations

This is a *short list* of authors and well-known speakers who have given me the inner reflection and inspiration to write this book.

Esther and Jerry Hicks, Abraham-Hicks publications: *Laws of Attraction, Ask and It's Given, The Vortex, The Astonishing Power of Emotions*

Eckhart Tolle, *The Power of Now* and *Stillness Speaks*

Neal Donald Walsch, *Conversations with God*

Howard Falco, *I Am*

Rhonda Byrne, *The Secret*

Jane Juska, *A Round-Heeled Woman*

Gail Sheehy, *Sex and the Seasoned Woman: Pursuing the Passionate Life*

Gangaji, *You Are That*

Jan Frazier, *When Fear Falls Away*

L. D. Thompson, *The Message: A Guide to Being Human*

Wayne Dyer, *The Shift*

Deepak Chopra, *The Seven Spiritual Laws of Success*

About the Author

Lori is a widow, but she doesn't like to define her life that way. This true story is one of hope, survival, and a resolve that transitioned her life of expectancy and control to one of waiting, observing, and appreciating. Through her transformation from grief to happiness, she shares the methods that helped her move on.

Lori is a daughter, wife, mother, career woman, and politician. Her life is not unique, just different than most. Her early experiences as a military brat instilled in her the ability to adjust to anything thrown her way.

She lives in northern California and has two grown children and three granddaughters. She is enjoying life to the fullest and now seeks happiness in everything. It is her hope that her story would assist anyone struggling with new widowhood or the midlife process of reimagining his or her own possibilities.